# DATE NIGHT COOKBOOK & ACTIVITIES FOR COUPLES

# Date Night
# COOKBOOK &
# ACTIVITIES
# FOR COUPLES

### Recipes and Games for a
### Romantic Night In

EDITED BY CRYSTAL SCHWANKE

CALLISTO PUBLISHING

To Ryan, who's always ready to humor this introvert's preference for a date night in, no matter how unusual the recipe or proposed activity.

# Contents

# Introduction

Hi! I'm Crystal, a happily married introvert who will choose a date night in over dinner and a movie almost every time.

Sometimes "getting away from it all" with your significant other doesn't mean going on a fancy vacation or out for a night on the town. It's tuning out the voices of other people so you can hear only each other and skipping the exciting visuals of a movie to create a magical evening together—just the two of you. There's no cacophony of voices or clinking glasses and silverware, no scheduling stress tied to reservations or babysitters. Conversation can flow, uninterrupted, and there's no need to "hold that thought" until a server leaves your table or until the credits roll on a movie that held you captive and mostly silent for two hours, other than the occasional whispered "Want more popcorn?"

I can hear you thinking, *Date nights in? Isn't that just "Netflix and chill" for the more established couple?* Au contraire!

These date nights in are much more engaging than any of that. Yes, you have to do some of the work because there's cooking involved, but you'll have your delightful sous-chef to help you (and maybe even keep your glass filled with the recommended beverage while they're at it). You're used to working as a team by now anyway, right?

The way it works is: You choose a theme from one of the chapters (Special Occasions, Staycation, A Date for Every Season, etc.) and then pick the menu that sounds best. Each menu will have a main and one or two sides plus a dessert or drink and a few extra tips you can use to take things up a notch, like a wine pairing. Don't worry: The recipes are uncomplicated, the amount of prep work is minimal, and the ingredients are easy to find.

If you thought this was just a cookbook, you're in for a surprise. I wouldn't leave you to fend for yourselves on the entertainment front! Sometimes you may get a question or two to ask your partner and get the conversation rolling. In other cases, you may have an activity, such as learning phrases from other languages to express your love.

If a menu speaks to you but you're not feeling the activity, go ahead and mix it up with an activity from another menu in the chapter. This is your night; I'll just be making suggestions so you don't spend the evening looking at each other and taking turns asking, "What do you want to do?" and responding, "I dunno. What do *you* want to do?"

I've even added ideas to keep your sous-chef busy so you won't fall into a situation where one person's doing all the cooking and the other one's just watching and keeping them company. I truly hope the menu pairings, working in tandem in the kitchen, and the activities will leave you feeling even more connected than before. Couples don't need extravagant experiences to weave a strong relationship—just connection that stems from a combination of conversation, creativity, playfulness, and teamwork. Delectable food doesn't hurt, either.

*Skillet Steak and Potatoes with Crispy Sage and Red Wine,*
**PAGE 64**

# CHAPTER ONE

# A Table for Two

Staying in doesn't have to be mundane. It can be even *more* romantic and lead to a better connection than a night out. There are so many perks to staying at home, such as creating a beautiful meal together and skipping the responsibility of finding a designated driver.

# DATE NIGHT AT HOME

When you find your groove in the kitchen, cooking together can feel like dancing together. You each move to the rhythm the recipe requires, chopping or mixing in your own space, focused, while also taking your partner's tasks into account. The result is a culinary masterpiece and a new level of connection based on communication, playfulness, and teamwork.

## Let's Stay In

True story: I used to despise cooking. I was completely intimidated by it, and the sheer thought of making anything more complicated than a salad or frozen meal brought on waves of panic and dread. Date nights in required takeout.

I finally decided that I needed to get over that and started branching out and cooking new things. Date nights in and cooking became especially important when we were budget-conscious new parents in an unfamiliar town where everything closed at 7:00 p.m.

Maybe you're in a similar situation: learning to make your own meals, or lacking extra wiggle room in the budget. In that case, when you sit down to eat, you will be celebrating not just your relationship but progress toward a goal!

Maybe you're busy combining two households into one, living in a new town with unfamiliar restaurants, or you just became empty nesters. Whatever your situation, creating a date night at home is always available and fun. All you really need are the dishes and appliances you already have, plus a trip to the grocery store.

## SAVINGS

Saving time and money is one of the most obvious benefits of a date night at home. You'll have to shop for groceries, but consider the time it takes to drive to a restaurant, wait for a table, wait for your food, wait to pay, and then drive home. You'll almost definitely save time when you stay in for the night. You can spend that extra time connecting with each other through an activity or uninterrupted conversation.

And the money you'll save when you buy the ingredients and cook them yourself? Quite a bit when compared with a dinner out at your favorite restaurant!

Transportation costs won't factor in, either (or the cost of a babysitter, if you have kids), saving even more time and money.

You can take the money you'd spend on a night out, tuck it away, and save it for a vacation or other big purchase instead.

## CONVENIENCE

My husband and I can't be the only ones who get analysis paralysis almost every time we decide to go out. We consider food, of course, but also ambiance, service, what's open, and how crowded the restaurant is likely to be. There are so many moving pieces in making a date night out work, it can end up being exhausting (the opposite of what you want).

It's more convenient to just choose your own menu, grab the groceries you need, and cook together. At home, it's not crowded, the atmosphere is whatever you want it to be, and you can even change into pajamas before dinner if you'd like.

## CUSTOMIZATION AND CREATIVITY

You can also perfect your menu when date night is at home. You won't have to stress about allergies or asking for your dish to be prepared a special way. If you really hate mushrooms (guilty!), you won't have to worry about those showing up in your meal. Think a certain herb or spice would make a nice addition to a recipe? Add it! You can have so much fun experimenting with different flavors in the kitchen.

### Make It a Date

Want to add a more complex dish to the menu than those you usually tackle at home? Plenty of people sign up for cooking classes and watch cooking shows or videos together to enhance their skills. You can take online cooking classes or follow a show or YouTube video as you work.

If you really want to impress each other, check out the menu you want to make ahead of time and watch videos to master new cooking skills. Instead of learning everything online the night of the date, you can learn from each other. (Showing off is just fun!)

## STAY UP LATE

You can go from dinner to bed in just a few minutes, so you can stay up enjoying each other's company without worrying about coordinating your schedule with a designated driver, public transportation, or a babysitter. You can even stay up until dawn if you want!

## SPEAKING OF . . .

Well, you're only a few steps away from your bedroom, so if you *do* want to go to bed early . . .

## Go for Game Night

With each menu, you'll get a game, activity, or question(s) to keep the conversation flowing. You'll discover new things about each other, express your love in new and creative ways, and have fun without distractions.

## AT-HOME ACTIVITIES

Don't worry, you won't need much for the activities and games. In most cases, you'll be fine with just a paper and pen—or no supplies at all. You can do the activities at home or anywhere else you happen to be staying.

## QUESTIONS

The questions you'll run across in the following chapters are meant to be thought-provoking, silly, fun, and nostalgic. Don't just answer and then stop talking—let the conversation flow from there. It's even more fun when you disagree. ("What do you mean, you'd rather live in New York than Paris?")

## MORE IDEAS TO MAKE YOUR OWN

If you come across an activity you don't want to do, questions you don't want to ask, or the rare activity that does require materials you don't have, just use what's listed as inspiration and go from there. You can always replace the activity with:

► Truth or dare

► Discussing songs you'd put on your make-out playlist

► Looking back at your first-date memories

► Learning your love language

- Sharing the first three things you'd buy if you won the lottery

- Playing "Would You Rather," the game where you each pose three questions—one silly, one normal, and one hard/real. Examples include: "Would you rather always be itchy or always have goose bumps?," "Would you rather vacation at the beach or in a city?," and "Would you rather have no kids or six kids?"

## Disconnect from Parent Mode

Hey, parents! If your kids are in bed or at their grandparents' house, now is your chance to challenge yourselves to disconnect from your parent roles and just focus on enjoying each other's company. Who can make it the longest without talking about the kids? Want to turn it into a drinking game where you have to take a sip every time one of you mentions them?

If nothing else, make sure all the toys and evidence of kiddos are out of sight and out of mind. Put the blocks away, shove the backpacks in a closet, and tuck the stuffed animals away on a shelf before you get started. Tonight is just about the two of you. Begin with quick shoulder rubs to start the relaxing evening off right, play your favorite slow song for a three-minute dance, or jump right into an activity, like planning your dream vacation.

# TWO COOKS IN THE KITCHEN

So, it's date night and you've decided to stay in and cook something delicious . . . together. If you're used to cooking alone, the thought of someone else in the kitchen with you might make you nervous. But don't worry, it'll be fun!

## Kitchen Setup

Setting up workstations and assigning tasks doesn't sound like the makings of a romantic evening, but it'll have you working together in a well-choreographed dance and ensure that everything goes smoothly.

If you have a work triangle—a layout that simplifies cooking—in your kitchen, decide who will do the washing (of produce and maybe even dishes, if you're cleaning and cooking at the same time), who will stand at the stove, and where the best spot to chop vegetables and open cans is. This will help you stay out of each other's way.

Even though the refrigerator is part of the work triangle, get everything you need for the recipe out and at the appropriate workstations first. If you don't have the work triangle setup or your kitchen space is small or galley-style, mise en place (getting all of the ingredients ready before you start) is especially important.

Don't forget the spices, measuring cups and spoons, and any tools you may need. I like to keep liquid measuring cups in the spice cabinet and the measuring spoons and dry measuring cups in the drawers just below that. It makes it easier to grab everything on my mental list and move to a different area in the kitchen if I need to.

In a small space, flirtatiously announce that you're nearby so you won't bump into each other until you want to. You *could* say something like "Behind you," but why not make it more fun with "Nice buns" or "Dancing cheek to cheek"? Discuss these phrases before you get started so there's no disaster while the other person is trying to figure out what you mean.

## Make It Fun

You're going to need some silliness to make this a date—not a chore—and keep both of you engaged, especially when you're waiting around for water to boil, cheese to brown, butter to melt, and so on.

If the recipe is simple—or if it becomes a one-person job after the first flurry of activity—one person can be designated chef while the other one is bartender or DJ. The chef is in charge, of course, but bartender has to keep the drinks topped off or the DJ has to keep the playlist fresh.

Speaking of which, before you get started, turn on music that speaks to your souls and makes it next to impossible not to dance together. You don't have to slow dance if that's not your style, but do keep your surroundings in mind. Don't get too enthusiastic and knock over a pot of boiling water or marinara sauce.

If you plan ahead, you could buy the most ridiculous aprons you can find for each other—or just buy one apron and then flip a coin to see who has to wear it (and possibly have their pic shared on social media for losing a bet).

## Tackle a Project Together

When you've had plenty of practice working together in the kitchen and have your routines down, it'll be time to challenge yourselves. Pick a cookbook with a cuisine that you're less familiar with and bookmark some recipes to try. Or learn a new skill: Try making sushi at home, prep a vegetable you've never made before, or create the perfect macarons in an unusual flavor.

# Cocktail Party for Two

The date-night menus all have tips on drink pairings, some alcoholic and some not. As you're setting up the ingredients for your meal, go ahead and get everything for your beverages, too. If the food recipes are relatively simple, the sous-chef's job may include bartending.

Not sure what to keep on hand to mix drinks at your home bar? Vodka or gin, citruses (orange, lime, and lemon are popular), a couple mixes (like Bloody Mary or daiquiri), tequila, sodas (like soda water, grapefruit soda for the Paloma [page 27] found on Taco Tuesday, or ginger beer for the El Diablo [page 143] in the Cold Nights, Spicy Food menu), bourbon or whiskey, light and/or dark rum, triple sec, agave syrup, and bitters would make a solid starting point.

Some tools you may need at your home bar include a knife, a citrus squeezer, a jigger, a bar spoon, a couple highball glasses, a couple rocks glasses, a cocktail shaker, and a strainer.

Don't feel like you have to go out and buy all these tools at once. Choose a drink the two of you would like to try, get the ingredients and tools for that, and then move on to the next one later. You'll build your collection as you go, eventually getting to a point where you just need to pick up a few specific ingredients every now and then.

Once you get the hang of mixing drinks, you may want to come up with your own Couple's Cocktail—a signature drink that combines your favorite flavors. When you do that, keep the ratio around 2:1:1 (2 parts alcohol, 1 part sweet, 1 part sour) for the best results. You can tweak that to your tastes a bit, but 2:1:1 is a good starting point.

# SHOPPING AND PLANNING FOR DATE NIGHT

Don't sweat it if the store is out of an ingredient you need. (I used to stress over this!) Simply check for a substitution or leave it out if it's just a small amount of something, like ¼ teaspoon of dried oregano. I promise that the recipes will still taste delicious even if you improvise a little.

## Smart Shopping

Shopping for two is different from shopping for a larger family. If you're just buying enough to cook for two, you may decide to splurge and opt for unusual-for-you ingredients for date nights (like a more expensive cut of meat). If you usually cook for kids most nights, combine those fancier ingredients with things your brood would turn their noses up at, like spices or unusual vegetables.

For some recipes, you may even decide to bump up the quality on some of the ingredients you usually wouldn't splurge on when shopping for regular meals. Be sure to try ripe, juicy heirloom tomatoes if you have the opportunity. If you've never had one, you'll be shocked by how much more flavor they have than the everyday tomatoes most people tend to buy when they're stocking up on groceries. One time, my husband and I visited a farmers' market before our date night and discovered rainbow carrots. They were new to us and especially pretty, cooked up just like regular carrots, and made dinner seem that much more special. Clearly, I'm *still* thinking about it!

Another thing you can do is choose smaller ingredients that pack the same flavor punch as something the recipe calls for (like a shallot instead of an onion). If you're normally big on using dried herbs, maybe now is your chance to buy the fresh stuff since you'll have less to chop.

You could also take this in a different direction and save money rather than splurging. Use this opportunity to shop for sales on two-packs of meat, or, if you see a good sale, buy a bigger package of meat that has just the right amount for your family plus two servings for your date night. Repackage the meat and freeze the extra for a future meal you cook for the whole family.

## Subbing In

As you make your shopping list with date night in mind, snap a quick photo of the recipes you'll be making and keep them readily available on your phone in case you need to make some quick changes at the store. That way, you'll be able to decide whether to substitute something else or skip an ingredient if something is out of stock. You can probably skip the ½ teaspoon of an herb or swap out one leafy green for another one, but having the recipe in your head or on your phone will help you make the right decision.

My hope is that this book won't load your pantry or spice cabinet with oddball ingredients you'll never use up or extra food you'll have to throw out. The recipes are designed for two, but depending on appetite, sometimes there will be leftovers to enjoy the next day. If you do find a recipe you want to share with others, feel free to multiply the ingredients and sub in more affordable (or bigger) options, like onions instead of shallots or regular tomatoes instead of heirloom.

The recipes use common ingredients, cooked up in a special way, so you can use the rest later. In some cases, you'll be able to freeze extra (for example, if you buy more meat than you need because it's on sale) and use it another night, saving money in the long run.

## Set the Mood

Don't skimp on the ambiance when you enjoy a date night at home. A fresh tablecloth, dancing candle flames, soft music that matches the theme, and fancy plates and silverware take the date from nice to special. But why stop there? Get creative and resourceful about it. Pretend you're the owner of the restaurant and you want to get the mood just right so your guests can't wait to return.

You could even take your meal to a different room or the deck. Sit on a blanket in the living room or use the coffee table while you sit on pillows. Pick some flowers or plants from the yard (they don't even have to be flowers—just something pretty and green!) and put them in a vase. Pull out the cloth napkins and set the table with your fancy spoons and extra forks even though you know you won't use them. It's all about presentation!

Tuck a coupon for dishwasher duty under the napkin and get dressed for dinner, whether that means fancy clothes or a matching pajama set.

# ABOUT THIS BOOK

Are you ready to get this date started? Here's what to expect.

## Menus

The menus all follow themes ranging from the romantic Anniversary Steakhouse Dinner (page 62) to the more casual Falling for Comfort Food (page 132) and Game Night Thursday (page 34). There is something for everyone with 20 menus featuring a wide variety of date-night favorites. With each menu, you'll get recommended meals (usually three recipes) that include a main dish, a side dish or appetizer, and a drink or dessert. In some cases, like the Big News, Big Flavors menu (page 81), you'll get a bonus recipe (this particular one has Honey Sriracha–Glazed Salmon, Zesty Romaine Salad, Corn Bread Muffins, and Ginger Limeade).

## For the Sous-Chef

As with any task involving more than one person, it's easy to end up in a middle-school group-project situation. You know what I mean—when everyone tries to do their own thing (or just watches) and hopes that everything will miraculously fall into place at the end. To avoid this unhappy outcome, enter the role of the sous-chef! Basically, a sous-chef is an assistant chef who helps prep the ingredients and fills in wherever else they're needed. Sometimes that means pouring a glass of wine for their partner once all the veggies are chopped and tossed into the pot!

You'll notice that almost all the recipes have tips for divvying up the tasks between the chef and sous-chef. Make sure each person gets to be chef and a chance to be sous-chef as you work your way through the book. If you see a recipe for your favorite dish, you may decide to take the lead. On the other hand, your partner might want to do most of the work and treat you to a lovely dinner featuring the foods you love most. Some recipes are just easier for one person to make, and that's okay, too. The sous-chef will still have tasks to take care of.

First time doing date night at home? Try the deceptively easy Taco Tuesday (page 23). It looks like a lot of work at first, but it's actually a fun and easy intro to date-night cooking.

## Labels

You'll see labels on the recipes that will help you narrow down your options based on how much time you have, what you're in the mood for, how much attention you want to give the cooking portion of your evening, and what you may have on hand.

- ▶ **5-Ingredient** for the recipes that have five ingredients (excluding basics like salt, pepper, and oil)

- ▶ **30-Minute** for recipes that you can prep and cook in 30 minutes or less

- ▶ **One Pot** for recipes made entirely in one pot or pan, like a Dutch oven, baking sheet, or cast-iron skillet

- ▶ **Vegetarian/Vegan** for recipes with limited or no animal products

## Tips

In some cases, I've provided extra tips to make your evening go more smoothly. Sometimes it'll be extra cooking or cleanup help so you're able to spend more time having fun. In other cases, there's information about the ingredients or suggestions for variations.

## Activities

With each menu, you'll find a game, activity, prompt, or question to take your date to the next level, but feel free to choose one from another menu, add your own, or use the recommendation as a starting point to create a whole new activity or spark conversation. Spice it up, make it sexier, customize it for your relationship and personalities, or even put money on the line.

*Garlic-Lime
Fish Tacos,*
**PAGE 24**

# CHAPTER TWO

# Date Night Every Night

Who says date nights at home can't happen throughout the week? You just need a plan and a couple recipes that are quick to make but don't necessarily feel like they are thrown together at the last minute. These are perfect because you get to enjoy each other's company without waiting in line or dealing with crowds.

# MEATLESS MONDAY

Meatless Monday is a classic, but for a fun date night, let's go beyond a giant salad or a vegetarian soup. I love this meal because it's hearty and unexpected, with a mix of textures to keep the meal interesting. If you've never replaced the beef (or turkey) in your burger with an earthy, slightly tangy portobello mushroom, you've been missing out on a fantastic flavor experience. I particularly like this menu most for the summer, because of the strawberry-basil sorbet at the end, but you can really enjoy it year-round, especially since the salad can be served warm or cold.

## MENU

*Crispy Eggplant Salad
with Halloumi Cheese*

*Roasted Balsamic
Portobello Mushroom
Burgers with Garlic Fries*

*Strawberry-Basil Sorbet*

## CHEERS!

I recommend a medium- to full-bodied red wine, like a Syrah or merlot. You could also try a Cabernet Sauvignon. If it's a beer you're after, a porter or stout is the way to go.

# Crispy Eggplant Salad with Halloumi Cheese

**SERVES 2 ♥ PREP TIME:** 15 MINUTES ♥ **COOK TIME:** 15 MINUTES

30-MINUTE, VEGETARIAN

If eggplant salad isn't a go-to dish in your house, I encourage you to put it on the list! Throw some sliced eggplant and halloumi cheese on the grill or in a pan, and add it to a bed of fresh greens for a starter hearty enough to be a main course, if you want a lighter meal. This dish can be served hot or chilled. As a cold salad, it offers an excellent make-ahead option. If one or both of you decide to prep this ahead of your date night, that'll leave you more time to dance, talk, or snuggle up under a blanket and look at the stars.

### FOR THE DRESSING

3 tablespoons red wine vinegar

1 tablespoon extra-virgin olive oil

1 garlic clove, finely minced

Salt

Freshly ground black pepper

### FOR THE SALAD

4 ounces halloumi, cut into 1/3- to 1/2-inch-thick slices

2 tablespoons vegetable oil

2 large eggs, beaten

1 cup unseasoned bread crumbs

1 small eggplant, cut into 1-inch-thick slices

2 cups salad mix (red butter lettuce, spinach, or other greens of choice)

2 small tomatoes, quartered

1 small cucumber, cut into small wedges

1. **To make the dressing:** In a small bowl, whisk together the red wine vinegar, olive oil, and garlic and season with salt and pepper.

2. **To make the salad:** Heat a nonstick skillet over high heat. Dry the halloumi cheese slices by blotting them with a paper towel. Transfer the slices to the skillet and cook for 1 to 2 minutes on each side, or until each side develops a deep brown crust, then set aside on a plate.

CONTINUED >>

**Crispy Eggplant Salad with Halloumi Cheese** CONTINUED

3. In the same skillet, heat the vegetable oil over medium-high heat. Pour the beaten eggs into one small bowl and the bread crumbs into another. Dip the eggplant slices in the eggs and then in the bread crumbs and place in the hot oil. Fry for 2 to 3 minutes on each side, or until golden brown. Drain on a paper towel–lined plate.

4. To assemble, divide the salad mix between two plates. Add the tomatoes, cucumber, halloumi, and fried eggplant. Drizzle with the dressing and serve.

**SWAP:** If you can't find halloumi, provolone (in a block, not pre-sliced) or any other grilling cheese will work as well.

**FOR THE SOUS-CHEF:** Dry the cheese for the chef to cook, then make the dressing.

# Roasted Balsamic Portobello Mushroom Burgers with Garlic Fries

**SERVES 2 ♥ PREP TIME:** 10 MINUTES ♥ **COOK TIME:** 20 MINUTES

30-MINUTE, VEGETARIAN

Portobello mushrooms are hearty, they won't fall apart when cooked, and they soak up any flavor you put on them. And what's a burger without fries? I've included a simple recipe for garlicky oven fries, too. The trick is to pop them in the oven before you start on the burgers, and they'll be done just in time.

Nonstick cooking spray

1 large russet potato, peeled and cut into thin strips

3 tablespoons extra-virgin olive oil, divided

1 teaspoon garlic powder

Salt

Freshly ground black pepper

2 portobello mushrooms, stemmed and washed

1 tablespoon balsamic vinegar, plus more for serving

1/4 cup jarred roasted red peppers

1/2 cup crumbled goat cheese

2 ciabatta buns

1 cup arugula leaves

1. Preheat the oven to 450°F. Line a baking sheet with aluminum foil and spray with cooking spray.

2. Spread the fries on the prepared baking sheet and drizzle with 1 tablespoon of olive oil. Sprinkle with the garlic powder, season with salt and pepper, and toss to combine. Bake for 20 minutes, stirring halfway through the cook time.

3. Meanwhile, drizzle the portobello mushrooms with the remaining 2 tablespoons of olive oil and the balsamic vinegar and season with salt and black pepper.

4. Put the mushrooms on a baking sheet and cook for 12 minutes, until they are soft. The fries will still be in the oven at this point.

CONTINUED >>

**Roasted Balsamic Portobello Mushroom Burgers
with Garlic Fries** CONTINUED

**5.** Remove the mushrooms from the oven and top with the roasted red peppers and goat cheese. Place the portobellos on sliced ciabatta buns and top with the arugula. Drizzle with additional balsamic vinegar. When the fries are done, remove them from the oven and serve alongside the burgers.

**TIP:** These portobello burgers are also great when made on the grill. Put the mushrooms on a grill or in a grill pan and cook for 12 minutes, watching closely so they don't burn.

**SWAP:** Use fresh baby spinach instead of arugula. You can also use fresh mozzarella instead of goat cheese.

**FOR THE SOUS-CHEF:** Preheat the oven and prepare the baking sheets. Once the fries are in the oven and the mushrooms are being prepped, start locating the toppings in the refrigerator or pantry so they're ready to go when the burgers are done.

# Strawberry-Basil Sorbet

**SERVES 2 ♥ PREP TIME:** 10 MINUTES

5-INGREDIENT, 30-MINUTE, ONE POT, VEGAN

Strawberries are an aphrodisiac, so this dessert is light, refreshing, *and* romantic. There's even a legend that says people who split a strawberry fall in love (and there are 1½ cups of strawberries to share here, so you're probably set for life). Also, there's no need for a special gadget to make this frozen treat: a high-speed blender or food processor makes quick work of it.

**1½ cups frozen strawberries**

**½ cup coconut water**

**1 tablespoon freshly squeezed lemon juice**

**1 teaspoon lemon zest**

**3 or 4 fresh basil leaves, chopped**

1. In a high-speed blender or food processor, combine the strawberries, coconut water, lemon juice, lemon zest, and basil. Blend until thick and smooth, scraping down the sides of the blender if needed.

2. Divide the sorbet between two bowls. Serve immediately.

**TIP:** You can use this recipe as a formula to make a variety of frozen treats with whatever frozen fruit you have on hand. Use coconut milk instead of coconut water for a thicker consistency, or mix in chocolate chips in place of the basil. The options are endless.

**FOR THE SOUS-CHEF:** Pull the ingredients out as the chef measures, then grab the bowls.

## ACTIVITY: How You See Me

Whether you're a natural artist or not, this activity will get your creative juices flowing. Either it'll be a masterpiece, or you'll love laughing at your perfectly imperfect creation—and what's better than that?

**Supplies needed:** Paper, pencils, or other drawing implements

**Estimated time:** 15 to 30 minutes (more, if you want to go the extra mile and pull out the paint)

### INSTRUCTIONS

1. Pull out a couple pieces of paper and pencils, pens, markers—whatever you have on hand.

2. Agree on a style of drawing if you'd like (caricature, still life, one-line drawing, stippling, etc.). If you want to go really simple, try contour drawing, where you don't look at the page and don't lift your pencil until you're done.

3. Take turns posing for each other's drawing.

4. Show each other your works of art.

5. Hang the drawings on the wall or refrigerator.

# TACO TUESDAY

If you love tacos and it's Tuesday (bonus if you love alliteration), this menu is a no-brainer! There's nothing better than sitting on a patio with your favorite person in the world, sipping a paloma or margarita, and enjoying a plate of fish tacos on a summer evening. Lucky for you, you don't even have to leave home to create the same experience, especially if you can dine outside. I love the way each recipe here ties in with the others. The grapefruit-avocado salad links the flavors of the paloma and tacos together perfectly.

## MENU

*Garlic-Lime Fish Tacos*

*Grapefruit-
Avocado Salad*

*Paloma*

## CHEERS!

Tequila's a go-to alcohol choice for taco nights, but if palomas aren't your thing, try just the lime juice and grapefruit soda on ice. Another option is to choose a lighter beer, like an IPA or pale lager. The crisp, bright flavors will pair well with the fish tacos. Wine lover? Choose a sauvignon blanc, a pinot grigio, or even a rosé.

# Garlic-Lime Fish Tacos

**SERVES 2 ♥ PREP TIME:** 10 MINUTES ♥ **COOK TIME:** 20 MINUTES
**30-MINUTE**

These tacos come together quickly, so you can take the extra time to get to know your partner even better. You can also get creative by adding garnishes that complement the mild fish with creamy fresh avocado and lime juice, spicy jalapeño peppers, and crunchy cabbage. Sometimes I'll add salsa or dress the cabbage in a little mayo and lime juice if I want some extra creaminess. There's a lot going on here with the textures and flavors. These tacos are kind of like a lot of good relationships—a mix of opposites that somehow just complement each other to create something beautiful.

**2 tablespoons extra-virgin olive oil, divided**

**½ small onion, chopped**

**2 garlic cloves, minced**

**Salt**

**8 ounces lean white fish fillets (such as cod, halibut, or tilapia)**

**Freshly ground black pepper**

**6 (6-inch) corn tortillas**

**1 cup shredded cabbage**

**1 medium avocado, sliced**

**2 teaspoons chopped fresh cilantro**

**2 jalapeño peppers, sliced (optional)**

**Chopped tomatoes, for garnish (optional)**

**2 tablespoons freshly squeezed lime juice**

1. In a skillet, heat 1 tablespoon of olive oil over medium heat. Add the onion and sauté for 4 to 5 minutes, until softened. Add the garlic and cook, stirring frequently, for 2 minutes. Sprinkle with salt. Mix well and set aside in a medium bowl.

2. Heat the remaining 1 tablespoon of oil in the skillet over medium heat. Add the fish and cook for about 5 minutes, flipping once or twice, until the flesh starts to flake. Season with salt and black pepper and set aside. With a fork, break the fish into large pieces and add to the bowl with the onion and garlic mixture, stirring to combine.

3. Heat a tortilla in the skillet or directly over the flame of a burner for 30 seconds to 1 minute on each side, or until warm and slightly browned. Repeat with the remaining tortillas.

**4.** To serve, put some cabbage on a warm tortilla. Top with the fish, avocado, cilantro, jalapeño peppers (if using), tomatoes (if using), and lime juice.

**TIP:** When summer fruits are in season, consider adding 1 cup of chopped mango or peaches to your tacos.

**FOR THE SOUS-CHEF:** Slice and chop the cabbage, avocado, jalapeño peppers, and cilantro while the chef sautés the onion and cooks the fish.

# Grapefruit-Avocado Salad

**SERVES 2 ♥ PREP TIME:** 20 MINUTES

5-INGREDIENT, 30-MINUTE, VEGETARIAN

It may sound like grapefruit and avocado have no business being in the same bowl, but this salad is the perfect example of how the simplest (even unexpected) ingredients can combine to make the most delicious dish. Prepare this salad when grapefruits are in season for the most flavorful results. It's tart, sweet, savory, creamy, and juicy all at the same time, making it an ideal side for the tacos.

| | |
|---|---|
| **1 ruby grapefruit** | **1 teaspoon honey** |
| **1 ripe avocado** | **1 small shallot, diced** |
| **1 tablespoon extra-virgin olive oil** | **Pinch salt** |
| **½ tablespoon white wine vinegar** | **Pinch freshly ground black pepper** |

1. Using your fingers, peel the grapefruit. With a sharp knife, carefully cut between the membranes to remove the grapefruit sections. Cut the avocado in half. Remove the pit. Remove the flesh from the skin using a spoon and cut into slices. Arrange the avocado and grapefruit on a plate or in a bowl in alternating slices.

2. In a small mason jar, combine the olive oil, white wine vinegar, honey, shallot, salt, and pepper. Stir with a whisk or cover with a lid and shake to combine.

3. Pour the vinaigrette over the avocado and grapefruit and toss to combine. Serve immediately.

**TIP:** Figuring out which avocado is ripe can be challenging. I like to give it a little squeeze—it should have some give, but not too much. Another indicator is the stem. If an avocado isn't too ripe, you should be able to peel off the stem, and underneath you should see green, not brown.

**SWAP:** No grapefruit around? You can use an orange instead. An orange will bring a little more sweetness to the dish, but the citrus will still pair nicely with the avocado.

**FOR THE SOUS-CHEF:** While the chef works on the salad, chop the shallot and mix the vinaigrette.

# Paloma

**SERVES 2** ♥ **PREP TIME:** 5 MINUTES

5-INGREDIENT, 30-MINUTE, VEGAN

The margarita is the United States' most popular tequila cocktail, but the paloma is Mexico's favorite. The sweet-and-sour combination of grapefruit soda, lime, and tequila or mezcal is easier to make than a margarita. The paloma's invention is often credited to Don Javier Delgado Corona, owner of La Capilla, a bar in Tequila, Mexico. Any tequila or mezcal works, but the smoky, earthy flavors of mezcal pair beautifully with crisp, slightly floral grapefruit.

**4 ounces tequila or mezcal**

**Juice of 1 lime**

**12 ounces grapefruit soda, chilled**

**Lime slices, for garnish**

Fill two highball glasses with ice. Pour in the tequila and lime juice and stir gently to chill. Top with the grapefruit soda and garnish with a lime slice.

**FOR THE SOUS-CHEF:** Why not offer to take this recipe on solo while the chef works on the grapefruit-avocado salad?

## ACTIVITY: **What Would You Choose?**

Get to know your significant other better while coming up with serious and absurd scenarios that involve choosing between two things. You may have played something similar before, since this kind of game is often used as an icebreaker at small gatherings. Write questions ahead of time or let questions come spontaneously.

**Estimated time:** 15 minutes or more

### INSTRUCTIONS

1. Take turns giving each other a choice between any two things. It could be anything, like general preferences or wacky situations you'd probably never find yourselves in. Here are a few examples to get you started:

   ▶ Mornings or evenings?

   ▶ Dancing or skipping everywhere you go (instead of walking) or singing every time words come out of your mouth?

   ▶ To never be able to wear socks again or never eat your favorite food again?

   ▶ Massage or cuddle?

   ▶ Square or circle?

   ▶ To have an iguana attached to your arm for a week or give up your phone for a month?

2. As your partner answers, feel free to ask about their decision-making process to gain insight into how their mind works.

3. Keep taking turns for as long as you like!

# BETTER THAN TAKEOUT WEDNESDAY

Sometimes it feels next to impossible not to cave and go for the takeout options, especially if you live in a place with an abundance of interesting restaurants, where the bold flavors of Indian food are just an online order away. Luckily, the Indian restaurant my husband and I love isn't nearly convenient enough to tempt us into an impromptu order. That means we have to make our own tikka masala and curry dishes most of the time. Once you try these recipes, you'll be glad you shared the experience of creating them with your partner instead of ordering in (at least this one time).

## MENU

*Chicken and Chickpea
Tikka Masala*

*Red Lentil Curry*

*Mint Lassi*

## CHEERS!

Go for a brown ale or Riesling with these dishes. The brown ale will give an earthy undertone to the dish, while a Riesling will add brightness and balance overall. Don't go too sweet with your drink here.

# Chicken and Chickpea Tikka Masala

**SERVES 2 ♥ PREP TIME:** 30 MINUTES ♥ **COOK TIME:** 35 MINUTES

Who needs takeout when you can whip up a delicious chicken tikka masala in about 45 minutes, in the comfort of your own home, while spending quality time with your special someone? Prepare for your kitchen to be filled with fragrant spices, as these bold flavors come together in a creamy sauce meant to be served over rice, another type of comfort food. If you both love dishes with a lot of flavor, this is a must-try.

**3 tablespoons masala paste, divided**

**½ cup plain Greek yogurt**

**8 ounces boneless, skinless chicken breast, diced**

**¾ cup canned chickpeas, rinsed and drained**

**¾ cup full-fat coconut milk**

**½ cup tomato puree**

**Sea salt**

**Cooked basmati rice, for serving (optional)**

**Fresh cilantro, for garnish (optional)**

1. In a medium bowl, stir together 1½ tablespoons of masala paste and the yogurt. Add the chicken and toss to coat evenly. Cover the bowl with plastic wrap or aluminum foil and refrigerate for 10 to 15 minutes to marinate.

2. Heat a large cast-iron skillet over medium-high heat. Put in the remaining 1½ tablespoons of masala paste and cook for 2 to 3 minutes, stirring frequently.

3. Add the chicken, ensuring that all the yogurt mixture from the bowl is added to the skillet, and cook for 5 to 8 minutes, stirring occasionally, until cooked through.

4. Stir in the chickpeas, coconut milk, and tomato puree. Simmer for 15 minutes. Season with salt and let stand for about 5 minutes, until the sauce begins to thicken. Serve with rice (if using) and garnish with cilantro (if using).

**FOR THE SOUS-CHEF:** Mix the masala paste and yogurt for the chef to marinate the chicken, then open the cans and rinse and drain the chickpeas.

# Red Lentil Curry

**SERVES 2** ♥ **PREP TIME:** 5 MINUTES ♥ **COOK TIME:** 20 MINUTES

30-MINUTE, VEGAN

Lentils are an excellent source of protein, so your whole meal gets an overall boost in protein when you prepare them as your side. You can serve this curry with naan, which is perfect for getting the last bit of sauce from your bowl. If you want to feed the family with leftovers, make a bigger batch and have this as your main dish later in the week.

| | |
|---|---|
| ⅓ cup white rice | 1 teaspoon ground cumin |
| 3 cups water | ½ teaspoon ground turmeric |
| ¾ cup red lentils | ½ teaspoon salt |
| ½ cup full-fat coconut milk | Juice of 1 lime |
| 1 tablespoon curry powder | ¼ cup chopped fresh cilantro |

1. In a small pot over medium-high heat, cook the rice according to the package instructions.

2. Meanwhile, in a medium pot over high heat, bring the water to a boil. Add the lentils and cook for about 10 minutes, stirring often, until soft. Drain the lentils if needed and return them to the pot. Add the coconut milk, curry powder, cumin, turmeric, salt, and lime juice. Stir well to combine.

3. Top the rice with the lentils and cilantro. Serve and enjoy.

**SWAP:** You can use brown or green lentils in the dish, but I prefer red lentils since they cook much faster. If you use brown or green lentils, add 10 minutes to the cooking time.

**FOR THE SOUS-CHEF:** While the chef is getting the rice and lentils going, open the can of coconut milk and measure out the spices so they're ready to be stirred in when the lentils are ready.

# Mint Lassi

**SERVES 2 ♥ PREP TIME:** 10 MINUTES

**5-INGREDIENT, 30-MINUTE, VEGETARIAN**

Mint turns this classic after-dinner, probiotic-rich yogurt smoothie into a cool, refreshing treat. You can add fruit that goes well with mint (I recommend mango) to make it even more interesting. Lassi has been around since roughly 1000 BCE and, according to Ayurvedic wisdom, may help calm the stomach and mind. (So it's perfect for a date night with a significant other who still gives you butterflies!)

**5 small yellow cardamom pods, seeded and pods discarded**

**2 tablespoons mint leaves, plus more for garnish**

**2 cups plain Greek yogurt**

**¼ cup sugar**

**Pinch kosher salt**

**1½ to 2 cups chilled water or milk**

**6 ice cubes (optional)**

1. In a mortar and pestle or spice grinder, grind the cardamom seeds to a fine powder, then add the mint leaves and grind as fine as possible.

2. Put the yogurt in a large mixing bowl. Using a whisk or an electric beater on low speed, beat the yogurt until it is completely smooth. Add the cardamom-mint mixture, sugar, and salt and blend well.

3. Add the chilled water (more or less, depending on how thick you like your lassi), and keep beating until the consistency is smooth and a frothy layer forms on top.

4. Put the ice cubes (if using) in tall serving glasses and pour the lassi over the ice. Garnish with mint leaves and serve immediately.

**TIP:** You can reduce the fat content by using low-fat or fat-free yogurt.

**FOR THE SOUS-CHEF:** Grind the cardamom seeds and mint leaves while the chef beats the yogurt.

## ACTIVITY: Word Associations

This is a fun and fast-paced game that can be done anywhere, but it's especially fun while you cook. Once you've played a few rounds during your date night, you might find yourself playing this game during a walk, on a car ride, over the phone, while doing chores around the house, or while spending time together on the couch.

**Supplies needed:** Timer (from an old board game or your phone)

**Estimated time:** As long as you'd like to spend on it

### INSTRUCTIONS

1. Set a timer for 1 minute.

2. One person says a random word. Then the other partner has to say the first word that comes to mind—no filters. The first player then says the first word that pops into their head.

3. Keep going back and forth until time is up. You never know where you'll end up, but you might find yourselves sharing stories between words for a chuckle. ("What? How did you get to *that* word from that one?") You can also continue this without a timer if you want to keep playing!

   Here's a quick example:
   Partner 1: Coffee
   Partner 2: Cup
   Partner 1: Cupcake
   Partner 2: Birthday

**TIP:** Add a rule to make things more challenging. For example, all words could have to fit into a specific category, start with the same letter, rhyme, and so on.

# GAME NIGHT THURSDAY

Whether you're watching a game on the couch or playing one at the table, you're going to want some snacks. In this case, you'll be enjoying an at-home spin on some fantastic bar foods. This menu boasts a variety of smoky, zesty, spicy, bright flavors, and even a touch of sweetness. It's just the laidback fare you need on a Thursday night. Kick back with nachos, sliders, and fries, as well as a whiskey drink that ties all the flavors together as if it were made for a modern menu like this instead of dating back to the 1800s.

## MENU

*Hawaiian-Style Chicken Sliders*

*Best French Fries with Chipotle Mayo*

*Adobo Turkey Nachos*

*Ginger Whiskey Buck*

## CHEERS!

This menu comes with a fun cocktail, but if you want something lighter, bar food goes perfectly with a beer. Try a hefeweizen to keep things light or even a brown ale. You could also mix 1½ ounces of light rum with 4 to 6 ounces of Coke over ice if you're not a beer fan. If you want to stay sharp for game play, skip the rum and squeeze some lime into your Coke instead.

# Hawaiian-Style Chicken Sliders

**SERVES 2** ♥ **PREP TIME:** 15 MINUTES ♥ **COOK TIME:** 15 MINUTES

30-MINUTE

What is it that makes sliders more fun than regular-size sandwiches? These chicken sliders are sweet, smoky, and cheesy—everything you want from a comfort food. The sweetness of the barbecue sauce is the perfect contrast to the saltiness of the provolone cheese. I feel like there are jokes to be made here about personality traits (sweet, cheesy, salty . . .), but I've got nothin'. Enjoy (your partner and the sliders)!

**1 boneless, skinless chicken breast, cut into 2 pieces**
**½ cup barbecue sauce**
**4 slider buns**

**4 slices provolone cheese**
**4 pineapple rings**
**½ cup shredded red cabbage**

1. Bring a small pot of water to boil over high heat. Add the chicken and boil for about 10 minutes, until cooked through. Remove the chicken from the pan. In a small bowl, shred the chicken and toss with the barbecue sauce.

2. Meanwhile, preheat the broiler.

3. Place one-quarter of the chicken on each slider bun bottom and top it with a slice of cheese.

4. Place the sliders on a baking sheet and broil for 1 to 2 minutes, until the cheese is melted.

5. Top each slider with a pineapple ring, shredded cabbage, and bun top. Serve and enjoy.

**TIP:** Using a precooked rotisserie chicken from the grocery store is a great way to save time with this recipe. Alternatively, if you have a little extra time, grill the pineapple slices for 2 to 3 minutes per side to give them more flavor and warmth.

**SWAP:** Use Swiss cheese instead of provolone for a more robust cheese flavor.

**FOR THE SOUS-CHEF:** Prep the toppings while the chef shreds the chicken.

# Best French Fries with Chipotle Mayo

**SERVES 2 ♥ PREP TIME:** 10 MINUTES ♥ **COOK TIME:** 30 MINUTES

5-INGREDIENT, VEGETARIAN

If you don't eat your French fries with mayo (or at least chipotle mayo), you're missing out. Treat each other to something delicious by frying up some potatoes and whipping up this quick sauce. These fries don't require a lot of effort, but they're so, so satisfying. The dipping sauce really puts them over the top and makes them the perfect partner to the sliders and nachos, as far as the flavor profiles go.

### FOR THE FRENCH FRIES

4 **cups vegetable oil**

2 **large russet potatoes, cut into ¼-inch sticks**

**Salt**

### FOR THE SAUCE

½ **cup mayonnaise**

4 **tablespoons minced chipotle in adobo**

2 **tablespoons freshly squeezed lime juice**

½ **teaspoon garlic powder**

**Salt**

**Freshly ground black pepper**

1. **To make the French fries:** In a Dutch oven, heat the oil over high heat. Once it's hot, dip the handle of a wooden spoon or a wooden chopstick into the oil to test the temperature. If the oil starts steadily bubbling, then it is hot enough for frying. If the oil bubbles very vigorously, then the oil is too hot and needs to cool a bit.

2. Gently put the potatoes in the oil and cook for 15 minutes without stirring. Use a pair of tongs to gently scrape loose any stuck potatoes after 15 minutes. Continue to cook, stirring when necessary, for 5 to 10 minutes, or until crisp and golden.

3. Using a large slotted spoon, remove the potatoes and spread them on a brown paper bag or paper towel–lined tray to cool.

**4.** Season with salt.

**5. To make the sauce:** In a small bowl, combine the mayonnaise, chipotle, lime juice, and garlic powder and season with salt and pepper. Mix well with a fork until well combined and smooth. Serve with the fries.

**TIP:** Have extra sauce? Use it to top Garlic-Lime Fish Tacos (page 24). It'll keep in the refrigerator for up to a week.

**FOR THE SOUS-CHEF:** While the chef cuts the potatoes, prepare the sauce.

# Adobo Turkey Nachos

**SERVES 2 ♥ PREP TIME:** 10 MINUTES ♥ **COOK TIME:** 15 MINUTES

30-MINUTE

Start your date off right with these nachos. They have the comfort food angle working for them because they're nachos, complete with cheese and a little bit of kick, but they also have veggies and turkey to round them out. Sautéing the slaw with the turkey makes it more flavorful and tender. Adobo is a great all-in-one Mexican seasoning blend. You can find it in the spice aisle at your grocery store.

1 teaspoon avocado oil

¼ cup diced onion

1 cup store-bought broccoli slaw

8 ounces lean ground turkey

1 teaspoon adobo seasoning

2 servings tortilla chips

1 cup shredded cheese of choice

1 cup seeded and diced tomatoes

1 cup chopped lettuce

2 tablespoons full-fat sour cream (optional)

1. In a medium skillet, heat the oil over medium heat until it shimmers.

2. Add the onion, broccoli slaw, and turkey. Allow the turkey to brown on one side, flip, and then break it up into crumbles. Sprinkle in the adobo seasoning and cook for 6 to 7 minutes, until the turkey is cooked through. Remove from the heat.

3. Meanwhile, preheat the oven to 300°F. Line a baking sheet with parchment paper.

4. Layer the tortilla chips on the prepared baking sheet. Spoon the turkey mixture on top of the chips, distributing evenly. Top with the cheese. Bake for 5 minutes, until the cheese is melted. Remove from the oven.

5. Top each serving with half of the tomatoes and lettuce, and 1 tablespoon of sour cream (if using).

**TIP:** Feel free to add salsa or guacamole in this recipe or create a nacho bar with your favorite ingredients, such as jalapeño pepper, red onion, and avocado.

**FOR THE SOUS-CHEF:** Chop the lettuce and tomatoes and get the tortilla chips on the baking sheet while the chef browns the turkey.

# Ginger Whiskey Buck

**SERVES 2** ♥ **PREP TIME:** 5 MINUTES

5-INGREDIENT, 30-MINUTE, VEGAN

The Whiskey Buck is spicy and smoky, thanks to the ginger beer and whiskey or bourbon, but there's a hint of tartness to it, too, from the lime. You can enjoy it any time of year and there's barely any prep time involved. I love it with this menu because of the way its flavors intertwine with the smokiness of the adobo nachos, brightness of the pineapple on the sliders, and the spiciness of the fries with chipotle mayo.

**3 ounces bourbon or rye whiskey**

**1 ounce lime juice**

**12 ounces ginger beer**

**2 lime wedges, for garnish**

Fill two mule mugs or highball glasses with ice. Pour half of the whiskey and lime juice into each and stir to chill. Top each drink with half of the chilled ginger beer and garnish with a lime wedge.

## ACTIVITY: Game On!

Game nights can often be better than movie nights, because they give you more of an opportunity to chat as you go—which means more time to connect with each other. (Try to do that while a movie's playing, and your partner might be a little less than enthusiastic about continuing the conversation.) Whether you spend the night watching a big game on television or pull out your old favorite board games and video games, make it an event. Even better, make it a fixed weekly event, so you can compile an always-changing stash of activities to keep things interesting.

**Supplies needed:** Your favorite board games and/or video games, plus your favorite candy, if desired

**Estimated time:** 3 hours or more

### INSTRUCTIONS

**Earlier in the week:**

1. Make a list of the games you want to play, including any childhood favorites.
2. Source any games you've been wanting to try.

**The night of:**

1. Grab your favorite board games, video games, and card games.
2. Flip a coin to see who gets to select tonight's game.
3. Spend the night competing against each other to win the most games.

**TIP:** Was your game collection tossed out a long time ago? Check thrift stores to see if they have old board games. Many classic video games are now available digitally if you no longer have the console or game cartridges to play. If you're hoping to play a game of Twister, there are even game spinner apps so you can play without a third person to spin the wheel.

# PIZZA NIGHT FRIDAY

Think pizza night has to be predictable? Not if you do it yourself! This date isn't your average pizza night. The meal might even leave you feeling inspired and energized, thanks to the bright flavors and vegetable-forward recipes. Don't worry, you still get a real crust to gnaw on and plenty of cheese (three kinds!), but they're complemented by a cauliflower topping that roasts in the oven until it's caramelized and flavorful. The combination of a sweet and tangy salad, this white pizza, and a couple light and bubbly Aperol spritzes makes this especially nice in the late spring or summer.

## MENU

*Peach, Prosciutto, Rocket, and Burrata Salad*

*Cauliflower and Ricotta Pizza*

*Aperol Spritz*

## CHEERS!

If you want something after you've finished your spritz, a crisp white wine or peach iced tea will pair well with the flavors in the salad and pizza.

# Peach, Prosciutto, Rocket, and Burrata Salad

**SERVES 2 ♥ PREP TIME:** 10 MINUTES

30-MINUTE, VEGETARIAN

I love a traditional Caprese salad (tomatoes, mozzarella, basil), but I think this one might just have it beat. Burrata is a style of fresh mozzarella that has a luxurious, creamy center. Paired with sweet peach, salty prosciutto, the slightly bitter bite of arugula—or the more fun "rocket," as they call it in the United Kingdom—and topped with a tangy sweet drizzle of balsamic vinegar and honey, it's like a sweet summer night in a bowl.

| | |
|---|---|
| **2 cups loosely packed arugula** | **1 peach** |
| **Juice of ½ lemon** | **4 prosciutto strips** |
| **2 teaspoons extra-virgin olive oil** | **1 (8-ounce) ball burrata cheese** |
| **Salt** | **1 tablespoon balsamic vinegar** |
| **Freshly ground black pepper** | **2 teaspoons honey** |

1. In a medium bowl, toss the arugula with the lemon juice and olive oil. Season with salt and pepper. Toss and arrange on a serving plate or in a serving bowl.

2. Cut the peach into eight wedges and place them on top of the arugula. Tear the prosciutto and arrange it among the arugula and peaches.

3. Tear the burrata and top the salad with it. Season the burrata generously with salt and pepper, then drizzle the entire salad with the balsamic vinegar and honey and serve family-style.

**SWAP:** If you can't find ripe peaches, you can try nectarines, cantaloupe, or even blackberries or cherries in this dish.

**FOR THE SOUS-CHEF:** While the chef completes step 1, slice the peach, tear the prosciutto, and unpack the burrata (but don't tear it yet, or the cream will seep out).

# Cauliflower and Ricotta Pizza

**SERVES 2** ♥ **PREP TIME:** 10 MINUTES ♥ **COOK TIME:** 45 MINUTES
VEGETARIAN

Making pizza at home makes for a fun date night, but that doesn't mean you have to make the dough from scratch and have a flour fight like in the movies. Instead, we opt for a premade dough (from the grocery store or your local pizza joint) and spend your time on the toppings. In this pizza, we amp up the cauliflower in a bright, salty marinade that pairs perfectly with creamy ricotta.

**All-purpose flour, for dusting**
**½ store-bought pizza dough ball**
**Juice of ½ lemon**
**2 garlic cloves, peeled**
**3 tablespoons capers, drained**
**2 tablespoons extra-virgin olive oil**
**Sea salt**

**Freshly ground black pepper**
**½ cauliflower head, cut into florets**
**¾ cup shredded mozzarella cheese**
**½ cup ricotta**
**½ cup unseasoned bread crumbs**
**¼ cup grated Parmesan cheese**

1. Preheat the oven to 400°F.

2. Dust a work surface with flour and place the pizza dough on it. Roll the dough into a 10-inch circle, ensuring the thickness of the dough is consistent. Transfer to a baking sheet and set aside.

3. In a blender or food processor, combine the lemon juice, garlic, capers, and olive oil. Season with salt and pepper, then blend until the ingredients form a loose paste.

4. Transfer the paste to a large bowl and add the cauliflower. Toss together, making sure all the florets are coated. Transfer to another baking sheet and roast for 20 minutes, or until the cauliflower is tender.

5. Turn up the oven to 525°F or as high as your oven temperature will go. Place the rack in the lower half of the oven.

**6.** Cover the pizza dough with the mozzarella cheese. Using a spoon, dot the top of the dough with the ricotta. Top that with the cauliflower mixture. Bake for 15 to 20 minutes, until the crust is golden brown.

**7.** Remove the pizza from the oven and carefully sprinkle the bread crumbs and Parmesan cheese on top. Return to the oven and bake for 3 minutes more.

**FOR THE SOUS-CHEF:** Prep the ingredients by chopping the cauliflower into florets. Then jump to step 3 and make the flavoring paste while the chef is rolling out the pizza dough. Work together in step 6 to add the toppings to the crust.

# Aperol Spritz

**SERVES 2** ♥ **PREP TIME:** 5 MINUTES

5-INGREDIENT, 30-MINUTE, VEGAN

Bright, bubbly, and not-too-sweet (you might even call it bittersweet!), the Aperol Spritz got its start in 1950s Italy and has traveled all around the world. It's the perfect refreshing addition to a dinner loaded with lighter flavors, especially if you're relaxing at home on a summer evening. You can enjoy it as an aperitivo (pre-meal drink) to prepare your stomachs for the delicious food to come or serve it with your pizza (or both!).

**2 ounces Aperol**

**3 ounces prosecco**

**1 ounce soda water**

**Orange slice, for garnish**

Fill two glasses with ice cubes. Add half of the Aperol to each glass and top with the prosecco and soda water. Stir gently to combine, and garnish with an orange slice.

## ACTIVITY: **Tell Me Everything**

Try interviewing your partner with these 10 questions. You may be surprised by some of the answers you get. If you make this menu again, feel free to come up with brand-new questions or use these again to dig a little deeper (you may each have more than one silly secret, for example).

**Estimated time:** 5 to 20 minutes

### INSTRUCTIONS

Take turns asking each other questions from the following list. Feel free to add your own questions at the end, as you like.

1. What is a silly secret you hide about yourself that you don't mind sharing with me?

2. What quirky or funny things do you tend to do when you're alone?

3. What is the theme song for your life?

4. What is your weirdest fear?

5. What's the most embarrassing moment you've ever experienced?

6. If you had to choose a career different from the one you're in (or currently planning), what would it be?

7. If you had to give up one of your five senses, what would it be and why?

8. If you could have any pet, what would it be?

9. If you could be another person for a day, whom would you choose?

10. Which food could you enjoy every single day for the rest of your life?

# COZY SATURDAY

This menu is the food equivalent of pulling your favorite sweatshirt out of the dryer on a chilly day and slipping it on while it's still warm. It's oh-so-cozy, thanks to the mac and cheese (with lobster!) and brownies à la mode. If you're looking for a meal to have before you snuggle up with your partner on a cold winter night, this is it. It's full of ooey, gooey comfort foods, plus roasted asparagus to balance out the rich flavors.

## MENU

*Baked Lobster Macaroni and Cheese*

*Parmesan Roasted Asparagus*

*Mug Brownies à la Mode*

## CHEERS!

A Chardonnay or Riesling will be perfect with the rich flavors of the macaroni and cheese. For beer, you can go either the brown ale route or the Saison (farmhouse ale) one. Add a splash of lavender syrup (a little goes a long way!) to lemonade for a nonalcoholic option.

# Baked Lobster Macaroni and Cheese

**SERVES 2 ♥ PREP TIME:** 10 MINUTES ♥ **COOK TIME:** 35 MINUTES

There's a certain harmony to the combination of this silky, creamy cheese sauce and rich, buttery lobster. The richness of the lobster marries well with the cheddar and Gruyère, and the crunchy bread crumb topping adds a wonderful contrasting texture. It's a perfect choice for when you want to wow your significant other with a decadent date night in.

Sea salt
8 ounces dry elbow macaroni
1 tablespoon unsalted butter
1 tablespoon all-purpose flour
¾ cup whole milk
Freshly ground black pepper
¼ cup shredded cheddar cheese

¼ cup shredded Gruyère cheese
¼ cup grated Parmesan cheese
4 ounces cooked lobster, chopped
2 tablespoons unseasoned bread crumbs
½ teaspoon extra-virgin olive oil

1. Preheat the oven to 375°F.

2. Bring a large pot of salted water to a boil over high heat. Cook the elbow macaroni according to the package directions, subtracting 1 minute from the cooking time. Drain and set aside.

3. In a large saucepan, melt the butter over medium heat. To create a roux, sprinkle the flour over the butter and cook for about 2 minutes, stirring constantly, until the mixture is golden in color.

4. Add the milk to the roux and whisk until combined. Season with salt and pepper. Simmer for about 2 minutes to allow the roux to thicken.

5. Remove the pan from the heat and whisk in the cheddar, Gruyère, and Parmesan cheeses, whisking until completely smooth.

6. Add the cooked pasta and lobster to the pan and stir until well combined. Spoon the pasta mixture into two ramekins, dividing evenly.

7. In a small bowl, stir together the bread crumbs and olive oil and season with salt and pepper. Sprinkle the mixture on top of each filled ramekin.

8. Bake the ramekins for 15 minutes, or until the cheese is bubbling and the bread crumbs are golden brown.

**SWAP:** Is one of you a seafood lover while the other could do without the lobster in this recipe? The noodles and cheese in this recipe make a perfect base for any protein. Sub in cooked chicken or bacon for a different flavor! (It also tastes great on its own, without any additions.)

**FOR THE SOUS-CHEF:** Preheat the oven and prep the ingredients by grating and shredding the cheeses and chopping the lobster. Help your chef get ready to put the macaroni and cheese in the oven by jumping ahead to step 7 to create the crunchy topping.

# Parmesan Roasted Asparagus

**SERVES 2** ♥ **PREP TIME:** 5 MINUTES ♥ **COOK TIME:** 10 MINUTES

5-INGREDIENT, 30-MINUTE, ONE POT, VEGETARIAN

Doesn't cheese just make everything better? Parmesan in particular is incredibly versatile and full of umami flavor. This sharp, salty, nutty cheese can be incorporated into a creamy pasta sauce, fried as a breading for your chicken cutlets, broiled on top of clams, and sprinkled over French fries. In this case, we use Parmesan to transform simple roasted asparagus into a savory masterpiece. The mixture of Parmesan, bread crumbs, and garlic powder is magical, trust me.

**1 bunch fresh asparagus, trimmed**

**1 tablespoon extra-virgin olive oil**

**1½ teaspoons unsalted butter, melted**

**3 tablespoons panko bread crumbs**

**4 tablespoons finely grated Parmesan cheese, divided**

**¼ teaspoon garlic powder**

**¼ teaspoon sea salt**

**¼ teaspoon freshly ground black pepper**

1. Preheat the oven to 425°F. Line a rimmed baking sheet with aluminum foil.

2. On the prepared baking sheet, combine the asparagus, olive oil, and butter and toss together to coat evenly. Spread the asparagus in a single layer.

3. Sprinkle with the bread crumbs, 3 tablespoons of Parmesan cheese, the garlic powder, salt, and pepper.

4. Roast for 8 to 10 minutes, or until the asparagus is crisp-tender and the cheese is melted.

5. Remove from the oven and garnish with the remaining 1 tablespoon of Parmesan before serving.

**FOR THE SOUS-CHEF:** The chef can snap off the ends of the asparagus while you preheat the oven, prepare the pan, and mix the Parmesan cheese, bread crumbs, garlic powder, salt, and pepper.

# Mug Brownies à la Mode

**SERVES 2** ♥ **PREP TIME:** 5 MINUTES ♥ **COOK TIME:** 5 MINUTES

30-MINUTE, VEGETARIAN

Microwaveable desserts-in-mugs are absolutely brilliant. This one is perfect for a date night like this because you'll be full and happy after the first two dishes, ready to settle down for the evening with something sweet. Simply stir a few ingredients together in a mug, and you can have dessert in seconds. This is so easy to make, a kid could do it (if you have kids, maybe you can teach them another day).

6 tablespoons sugar

6 tablespoons all-purpose flour

6 tablespoons cocoa powder

⅛ teaspoon sea salt

¼ cup semisweet chocolate chips

3 tablespoons unsalted butter, melted

⅓ cup milk

½ teaspoon vanilla extract

Vanilla ice cream, for serving

1. In each of two mugs, stir together 3 tablespoons of sugar, 3 tablespoons of flour, 3 tablespoons of cocoa powder, and half of the salt. Add 2 tablespoons of chocolate chips and stir until the chips are distributed throughout.

2. To each mug, add 1½ tablespoons of butter, half of the milk, and ¼ teaspoon of vanilla. Using a small spatula, stir just until the ingredients are combined.

3. One mug at a time, microwave on high for 1 minute. Check on the brownie, microwave it for 15 seconds, and check on it again. Microwave for 15 more seconds or until a toothpick inserted in the center comes out clean. Top with vanilla ice cream and serve.

**FOR THE SOUS-CHEF:** The beauty of this recipe is that each person assembles their own mug brownie!

# ACTIVITY: Pay Extra Attention

How well do you pay attention to each other and the world around you? (Hopefully pretty well, especially while you're cooking together in the kitchen!) You can play this pop quiz anywhere, as long as you're together.

**Supplies needed:** Pencil and paper

**Estimated time:** 2 minutes to 1 hour

## INSTRUCTIONS

1. See how observant your partner is by asking them questions about your environment, other people, or maybe even yourself. If you've been together for a while and questions about each other and your surroundings would be too easy, use a movie or television show as the subject for this game.

2. Take turns asking each other questions. Correct answers get a point, and you can keep score with a piece of paper and pencil.

3. You need to be able to verify an answer without giving your partner a chance to peek. For example, if you ask what color your socks are, hide your feet right before asking. Or, pause the movie and ask what was on the counter behind a certain character, then rewind it to see if your partner was right.

# SUNDAY BRUNCH

While this menu is suggested as a leisurely Sunday meal, it works just as well on a free Wednesday morning, a Thursday night, or whenever that brunch-for-dinner mood strikes. If you have kids who spent the night at the grandparents' or a friend's house, you can enjoy these dishes after sleeping in for the first time in ages. (Doesn't that feel glorious?) I especially love this menu because it looks and tastes like it requires more effort than it does. Another beautiful thing about these recipes is that they are just as wonderful in the summer as in the winter.

## MENU

*Puff Pastry Eggs
with Cheese*

*Sweet Potato and
Bacon Hash*

*Bloody Mary*

## CHEERS!

Not a Bloody Mary fan? You can always go the mimosa route by combining equal parts champagne and orange juice with a little orange liqueur. Add strawberries or cherries to make it fancy. Or try a virgin "tequila" sunrise by mixing 5 ounces of orange juice and an ounce of grenadine.

# Puff Pastry Eggs with Cheese

**MAKES 4 PASTRIES** ♥ **PREP TIME:** 15 MINUTES ♥ **COOK TIME:** 30 MINUTES

5-INGREDIENT, VEGETARIAN

My husband and I used to regularly go out for brunch, but I never liked the idea of getting up early enough to beat the crowd. We started learning how to make brunch foods at home so we could make easy weeknight or weekend feasts. These elegant little bites—with crispy edges of flaky pastry and a soft-baked egg with cheese—are actually quite simple.

1 frozen puff pastry sheet, thawed
Butter, for greasing
4 large eggs
½ cup shredded cheddar cheese

Salt
Freshly ground black pepper
Fresh thyme, for garnish (optional)

1. Preheat the oven to 400°F. Line a baking sheet with parchment paper.

2. Using a rolling pin, lightly roll out the puff pastry so it is in a rough square shape (it doesn't have to be perfect) of an even thickness and the creases have been smoothed out. Cut the dough into four pieces, slicing in half once lengthwise and once crosswise.

3. Put each piece of pastry on the prepared baking sheet. Grease or butter the outside bottom of four oven-safe ramekins or any small oven-safe dish, and place one in the middle of each piece of pastry. Transfer the baking sheet to the oven. Bake the pastries with the ramekins sitting in the middle for 10 minutes, or until the edges have puffed up around the ramekins, creating a well for each egg. Remove the baking sheet from the oven, and, using hot pads or oven mitts, remove the ramekins.

4. Gently crack an egg into the center of each pastry, in the hollows formed by the ramekins, and sprinkle each with the cheese. Season each with a pinch of salt and pepper.

5. Transfer the baking sheet to the oven and bake for 15 to 20 minutes, or until the eggs are cooked to your liking. Remove from the oven. Garnish with thyme (if using).

**SWAP:** For a flavor variation, try sliced cherry tomatoes, some pesto, and plenty of freshly grated Parmesan cheese on top.

**FOR THE SOUS-CHEF:** While the chef prepares the pasty, gather the ramekins and make sure the non-pastry ingredients are in place and ready to go when the pastry comes out of the oven the first time.

# Sweet Potato and Bacon Hash

**SERVES 2** ♥ **PREP TIME:** 10 MINUTES ♥ **COOK TIME:** 20 MINUTES
**30-MINUTE**

This is one of my go-to meals for brunches and for dinners. Many times, I will use whatever vegetables I have in our refrigerator, but the sweet potato and kale in this version make my favorite combination, especially in the fall. I love how the crispy, salty bacon; creamy sweet potatoes; and slightly bitter, hearty kale combine. If the pastries are enough eggs for you, feel free to omit the fried eggs here.

3 bacon slices, cut into
   small pieces
1 medium sweet potato, peeled and
   cut into ½-inch dice
1 shallot, diced
2 garlic cloves, minced

3 large Tuscan kale leaves,
   stemmed and chopped
½ teaspoon salt
¼ teaspoon freshly ground
   black pepper
2 large eggs

1. In an 8- or 9-inch cast-iron skillet, cook the bacon over medium-high heat for about 5 minutes, until crispy. Remove from the skillet, leaving about 2 tablespoons of bacon grease in the skillet.

2. Add the sweet potato, shallot, and garlic to the skillet. Cook for about 10 minutes, until the sweet potato is softened.

3. Add the kale to the skillet and stir to combine with the other ingredients. Add the salt and pepper.

4. In a small nonstick skillet over medium-high heat, crack the eggs. Cook the eggs for 1 to 2 minutes on each side, until they reach the desired consistency.

5. Divide the hash between two plates and top with the eggs. Serve immediately.

**FOR THE SOUS-CHEF:** While the chef cooks the bacon, chop the veggies so they're ready to go into the skillet when it's time. If the chef doesn't mind, you can cook the eggs while they cook the kale to make things come together as quickly as possible.

# Bloody Mary

**SERVES 2** ♥ **PREP TIME:** 5 MINUTES

30-MINUTE, VEGAN

You and your partner probably don't agree on everything, and that might even include how to make the best Bloody Mary. Use this recipe as a guide but feel free to play around with the ingredients until you've created the perfect Bloody Mary for your own tastes.

## FOR THE MIX

**16 ounces tomato juice or tomato and vegetable juice blend**

**¾ teaspoons Worcestershire sauce**

**¼ teaspoon hot sauce**

**¼ teaspoon black pepper**

**1 pinch celery salt**

**Prepared horseradish (optional)**

## FOR THE DRINKS

**4 ounces vodka**

**1 ounce freshly squeezed lemon juice**

**Cornichons and lime slices, for garnish**

1. **To make the mix:** Combine the tomato juice, Worcestershire sauce, hot sauce, pepper, celery salt, and horseradish to taste (if using) in a large pitcher, and stir thoroughly.

2. **To make the drinks:** Fill two highball or pint glasses with ice cubes. Add half of the vodka, lemon juice, and mix to each glass and stir several times to chill. Garnish with cornichon.

**TIP:** When garnishing a Bloody Mary, you don't have to stop at a lone celery stalk. It's common to see them garnished to the nines with savory and spicy finger foods. This recipe makes fairly large drinks (with a high ratio of vegetable juice mix to alcohol), so feel free to pour them into extra-large glasses and fill up the rims with fun ingredients!

**FOR THE SOUS-CHEF:** If you're using a variety of garnishes—like cocktail onions and fresh cherry tomatoes— with your cornichons, you can slide them all onto toothpicks.

*Bloody Mary,*
**PAGE 57**

## ACTIVITY: **Memories Around Us**

This simple game will take you down memory lane with your significant other. You may even be surprised by what tiny details they remember about your life so far as a couple. At first it may sound easy. After all, shouldn't everything in your home remind you of each other? Go deeper, though, and wow each other.

**Estimated time:** Varies (as long as you'd like to play or until you run out of ideas!)

### INSTRUCTIONS

Look around the room for items that remind you of a shared memory. The item doesn't have to be a souvenir from a trip, a gift, or a memento from a special occasion. It could be anything—the more random the better. Grab the item and then reminisce with your partner about "that time we/ you/I . . ." Then it's their turn to do the same. If you want to make things even more interesting, you could hold the item up and see if your partner comes up with the same memory you did.

*Prosecco Ice Pops,* **PAGE 71**

# CHAPTER THREE

# Special Occasions

Sometimes waiting for a table at a popular
restaurant, trying to flag down a waiter on a
busy night, or just getting downtown and back
can turn a celebration into a night full of stress.
Instead, try one of these elegant menus and enjoy a
quiet night alone with your partner. Dress up, turn
on some soft piano music, light candles (or start a
roaring fire in the fireplace if it's cold), and
soak in the moment.

# ANNIVERSARY STEAKHOUSE DINNER

Ah, the steakhouse dinner. It's a classic choice when you have something to celebrate, so of course I had to include it here. Skip waiting in line for a table, avoid feeling like you need to yell over the din of a restaurant, and enjoy this meal with a glass of wine or a classic cocktail. You'll be able to cook the steaks to suit your preferences (instead of having to guess if the restaurant's standards meet yours), and you won't want to miss out on the way the zesty kale Caesar salad balances the sage and honey flavors of the steak and potatoes.

## MENU

*Kale Caesar Salad*

*Skillet Steak and Potatoes with Crispy Sage and Red Wine*

*Molten Chocolate Lava Cakes*

## CHEERS!

This meal begs for a red wine. Try a full-bodied red like cabernet sauvignon or a dry, light- to medium-bodied Pinot Noir. I would choose heavier, smokier, more tannic wines over the lighter, fruity, sweet ones to best complement the flavors in this meal.

# Kale Caesar Salad

**SERVES 2** ♥ **PREP TIME:** 15 MINUTES ♥ **COOK TIME:** 10 MINUTES
**30-MINUTE**

I've been obsessed with kale since I discovered it around 10 years ago, and it's assertive flavor stands up wonderfully to the strong zing of a Caesar dressing. Adding romaine lettuce breaks up the stronger flavor and heartier texture a bit and gives it a more traditional note. Working the dressing into the leaves and giving it time to soak up all the flavor will also help soften the kale's texture.

1 cup cubed baguette

2 tablespoons extra-virgin olive oil, plus ¼ cup

Salt

Freshly ground black pepper

2 teaspoons Dijon mustard

2 teaspoons Worcestershire sauce

½ teaspoon hot sauce

2 teaspoons anchovy paste

1 cup grated Parmesan cheese, divided

1 bunch Tuscan kale, stemmed and finely chopped

1 head romaine lettuce, chopped

1. Preheat the oven to 400°F. In a medium bowl, toss the bread cubes with 2 tablespoons of olive oil and season with salt and pepper. Place them on a baking sheet and bake for 10 minutes.

2. In a small bowl, whisk together the remaining ¼ cup of olive oil, the Dijon mustard, Worcestershire sauce, hot sauce, anchovy paste, and ½ cup of Parmesan cheese.

3. In a medium bowl, combine the kale and romaine. Drizzle with the dressing and stir well for at least 2 minutes to incorporate the dressing into the leaves. Let sit for 5 to 10 minutes.

4. Top with the remaining ½ cup of Parmesan cheese and croutons. Serve and enjoy.

**SWAP:** Omit the anchovy paste if you can't find it or don't care for the salty, oily fish. You can also use bagged croutons if you don't want to make them.

**FOR THE SOUS-CHEF:** Whisk up the dressing while the chef is making the croutons.

# Skillet Steak and Potatoes with Crispy Sage and Red Wine

**SERVES 2** ♥ **PREP TIME:** 5 MINUTES ♥ **COOK TIME:** 40 MINUTES

Everyone should have a go-to meat-and-potatoes dish, and this one is simple enough for beginners to love, mainly because tenderloin is hard to screw up (no stress allowed on date night!). You could also use sirloin and hanger cuts, but with these flavors of red wine, sage, and honey, filets mignons are just right. I love how the potatoes crisp up and play well with the asparagus side, too.

2 tablespoons butter, divided

2 (4-ounce) filets mignons

Salt

1 cup red wine

2 tablespoons honey

1 tablespoon extra-virgin olive oil

2 medium potatoes, peeled and diced

5 or 6 fresh sage leaves

1. In a large heavy-bottomed skillet, melt 1 tablespoon of butter over medium-high heat. Sprinkle each filet with a large pinch of salt and sear for 2 to 4 minutes on each side, or until they reach the desired level of doneness. Transfer to a plate or cutting board and let rest.

2. Deglaze the skillet with the red wine, scraping the bottom to lift off any browned bits left over from the steak. Continue to stir over medium-high heat while drizzling in the honey. Simmer for 10 to 15 minutes, or until the sauce is reduced by half. (If you like a thicker sauce, you can sprinkle in a little arrowroot powder or cornstarch and whisk the sauce over medium heat until thickened.) Pour the sauce into a small serving bowl.

3. Combine the remaining 1 tablespoon of butter and the olive oil in the skillet. When the butter and oil are hot, add the potatoes with a large pinch of salt. Cook the potatoes for about 10 minutes, or until crisped on all sides and tender. Add the sage and let it crisp in the oil. Slice the steak and add it back to the skillet for 2 to 3 minutes, or just long enough to heat. Remove from the heat.

4. Plate the potatoes and steak. Serve the red wine–honey sauce on the side or drizzled over the steak.

**TIP:** They say to cook only with wine that you would drink. I do have to agree here. Skip the cooking wine, and just donate a glass of what you and your partner are drinking that evening to the cause. Alternatively, I have been known to put a cork in a bottle of unfinished wine and keep it in the refrigerator for future cooking; if it was once drink-able, it is acceptable for cooking, in my book.

**FOR THE SOUS-CHEF:** Peel and dice the potatoes while the chef cooks the steak and makes the sauce.

# Molten Chocolate Lava Cakes

**SERVES 2 ♥ PREP TIME:** 10 MINUTES ♥ **COOK TIME:** 15 MINUTES

30-MINUTE, VEGETARIAN

The more decadent a chocolate dessert is, the happier I am. If you're a chocolate lover like me, you really can't go wrong with these lava cakes. I particularly like to top these cakes with ice cream, but you could also opt for salted caramel and powdered sugar. You can customize these by having different flavors of ice cream and other toppings on hand in case one person is less chocolate obsessed than the other.

Nonstick cooking spray

4 tablespoons unsalted butter

½ cup semisweet chocolate chips

½ cup powdered sugar

¼ teaspoon salt

1 large egg

½ teaspoon vanilla extract

¼ cup all-purpose flour

Ice cream, salted caramel, or additional powdered sugar, for serving (optional)

1. Preheat the oven to 425°F. Lightly coat two ramekins with nonstick cooking spray.

2. In a microwave-safe bowl, combine the butter and chocolate chips. Microwave in 20-second increments, stirring well between each session. Repeat until melted, about 1 minute.

3. Add the powdered sugar and salt and whisk well. Add the egg and vanilla, whisking again. Stir in the flour, mixing until just combined. Divide the batter between the prepared ramekins.

**4.** Bake for 10 to 12 minutes, until the cake is puffed but the center isn't set.

**5.** If using, top with ice cream, salted caramel, or powdered sugar and serve.

**TIP:** Many recipes for molten cake call for chopped chocolate, but I think chocolate chips work just as well. Plus, using chips saves time because you don't have to do all that chopping.

**SWAP:** If you want to turn up the decadence, swap in dark chocolate chips. They have more cacao and add an even deeper, richer flavor to this dessert.

**FOR THE SOUS-CHEF:** This is really a recipe for one person to make. Go ahead and clean the kitchen while the chef whips them up—less work later!

## ACTIVITY: Blockbuster Love

Imagine that Steven Spielberg is sitting at your dinner table. This could be your BIG break! Pitch a movie about your love story complete with a title, a tagline, a description, and characters. Get creative! Which celebrities would you and your partner cast as yourselves? Why did you choose them?

# INTIMATE VALENTINE'S DINNER

Going out with your special someone on Valentine's Day sounds romantic, but it can often come with a long wait (yes, even with reservations), and a rigid, pricey prix fixe menu. It's far more fun to enjoy a fondue dinner for two at home, bookended by a sweet and tangy pecan and pear salad and an unusual dessert. Plus, no restaurant you'd go to would offer you Prosecco ice pops for dessert, so that's an extra advantage here. If fondue sounds intimidating, don't worry! It's easier to make at home than you might think.

## MENU

*Pecan and Pear
Arugula Salad*

*Fondue for Two*

*Prosecco Ice Pops*

## CHEERS!

Valentine's Day calls for bubbles—and lots of them. You can make a quick champagne cocktail by adding a sugar cube and a few drops of Angostura bitters to any dry sparkling wine. If an effervescent cider is more your speed, add a splash of pomegranate juice for some rosy color and extra flavor.

# Pecan and Pear Arugula Salad

**SERVES 2** ♥ **PREP TIME:** 15 MINUTES ♥ **COOK TIME:** 10 MINUTES

30-MINUTE, VEGETARIAN

Salads can be so much more than chopped lettuce and cherry tomatoes, even when they aren't the main course. The key to a satisfying salad is incorporating a variety of textures into every bite. With toasted pecans, crisp pears, and creamy goat cheese, this salad is a scrumptious side for a steak dinner. If you have leftovers, they'll make a great lunch with grilled chicken on top. Set any extra aside and don't toss it with the dressing until you're ready to serve.

½ cup pecan halves

2 tablespoons red wine vinegar

1 tablespoon extra-virgin olive oil

1 tablespoon whole-grain mustard

1 tablespoon honey

3 cups arugula

1 pear, sliced

¼ cup crumbled goat cheese

1. In a small cast-iron skillet, toast the pecans over low heat until fragrant, about 5 minutes.

2. In a small bowl, whisk the red wine vinegar, olive oil, mustard, and honey.

3. Divide the arugula and top with the pear, pecans, and goat cheese. Drizzle with dressing and toss to coat.

**FOR THE SOUS-CHEF:** Slice the pear and make the dressing while the chef is toasting the pecans.

# Fondue for Two

**SERVES 2 ♥ PREP TIME:** 20 MINUTES ♥ **COOK TIME:** 10 MINUTES

30-MINUTE, ONE POT, VEGETARIAN

There is nothing more comforting, classic, and, I suppose, a bit old school than a great fondue. The first time I tried it, my husband and I were on a romantic date in Atlanta. I loved dipping different foods into the hot, gooey cheese. There's a dipper here for everyone, from potatoes and radishes to hunks of bread and sausage. This dish is a celebration in a pot.

4 ounces firm Alpine cheese, such as Gruyère or Comté

4 ounces Gouda cheese

4 ounces Fontina cheese

1 tablespoon cornstarch

²⁄₃ cup dry white wine

1 garlic clove, minced

1½ teaspoons freshly squeezed lemon juice

1½ teaspoons brandy

½ teaspoon Dijon mustard

Pinch freshly grated nutmeg

Dippers of choice, such as potatoes, radishes, bread, or sausage

1. Grate the Alpine, Gouda, and Fontina cheeses into a medium mixing bowl. Add the cornstarch and toss to thoroughly coat.

2. In an oven-safe fondue pot or a heavy-bottomed small Dutch oven or skillet, bring the wine, garlic, and lemon juice to a simmer over low heat. Add the cheese in thirds, stirring to ensure that each third is melted and whisked smooth before adding the next. Add the brandy, mustard, and nutmeg. Stir to incorporate. Remove from the heat.

3. Arrange bite-size dippers on a platter. Serve with skewers or forks. Dip into the cheese, and enjoy.

**TIP:** A fondue pot is great, but a heavy cast-iron pan or Dutch oven will also do the trick when making this dish for two, since they retain enough heat to keep the cheese melty while you eat.

**FOR THE SOUS-CHEF:** Grating cheese is a lot of work! Go ahead and jump in to help with this task. Once all the cheese has been grated, toss it with cornstarch while the chef brings the wine, garlic, and lemon juice to a simmer.

# Prosecco Ice Pops

**MAKES 4 ♥ PREP TIME:** 10 MINUTES, PLUS 8 HOURS TO FREEZE

5-INGREDIENT, VEGAN

Not every date night has to end with dessert, but these prosecco ice pops are a good way to enjoy a boozy little treat. Since this is an outdoors, summertime-friendly meal, why not make it especially refreshing? If you don't have ice-pop molds, use paper or plastic cups or ice cube trays. Fill them, place plastic wrap on top, and gently poke a hole through the wrap with an ice-pop stick. Freeze for a few hours, then wiggle the pops out and enjoy.

¾ cups strawberries

¾ cups chopped mango

Juice of ½ lemon

¼ cup simple syrup

1 (750 mL) bottle prosecco, divided

1. In a high-speed blender, combine the strawberries, mango, and lemon juice. Blend until smooth.

2. In a large bowl, combine the fruit puree, simple syrup, and half of the bottle of prosecco. Let stand until the bubbles from the prosecco subside.

3. Pour the mixture evenly into ice-pop molds. Insert an ice-pop stick into each mold. Freeze for 8 hours or overnight.

4. To serve, place the pops upside down in glasses and add prosecco to each glass.

**TIP:** To make your own simple syrup, combine equal parts (say, 1 cup each) sugar and water in a small saucepan over medium heat. Heat until the sugar dissolves. Cool and keep refrigerated for up to 2 weeks.

**FOR THE SOUS-CHEF:** Make the simple syrup (if not using store-bought) while the chef chops the fruit and blends it up.

## ACTIVITY: Love Letters

Whether you're starting out in a new relationship or you've been together for a long time, communicating how you feel about each other is paramount.

**Supplies needed:** Pen and paper

**Estimated time:** 15 to 30 minutes

### INSTRUCTIONS

Take the time to reflect on your affection for your partner by writing them a love letter. Here are some prompts and tips:

▶ Reflect on at least three of your favorite memories of your partner and/ or your relationship. Share why these memories are your favorites.

▶ Include at least 10 things you like about your partner. It could be their beautiful eyes, their outgoing personality, or their gentle nature.

▶ Tell your partner what your hopes and dreams are for the two of you as a couple. What does your future look like in your heart and mind?

▶ Write about what makes your partner unique to you from anyone else you dated before. Have them do the same with you.

▶ Make your love letters as intentional and detailed as you possibly can. This is an opportunity to put your heart and soul on the page for your partner to read and reread.

This date lends itself perfectly to sharing and receiving words of affirmation. You can also snuggle up to each other on the couch and read your love letters out loud. Follow it up with a make-out session if the mood takes you! Make an agreement to write new letters at least once a year (and perhaps on your anniversary or another special occasion).

# BIRTHDAY BISTRO

Happy Birthday! It's time to celebrate that special day with your special someone. For this meal, turn your home into a French bistro with classic mussels, a hearty chickpea and green bean salad, and the most important French element—some good, crusty bread. And for dessert, stick a candle through the crackly crust of a coffee crème brûlée. This menu is designed to hit the spot no matter what time of year you were born.

## MENU

*Mussels in White Wine and Garlic with Crusty Bread*

*Roasted Chickpea and Green Bean Salad*

*Coffee Crème Brûlée*

## CHEERS!

Go ahead and pour two glasses of the wine you're cooking with, if you'd like. You could also enjoy these dishes with a Riesling or pinot grigio that's a little sweeter than the wine you're cooking with, if that's more your taste. Another option? A white ale (very bistro friendly), or a classic Perrier.

# Mussels in White Wine and Garlic with Crusty Bread

**SERVES 2** ♥ **PREP TIME:** 10 MINUTES ♥ **COOK TIME:** 15 MINUTES

**30-MINUTE, ONE POT**

Here's a twist on mussels mariniere, or *moules marinières*, a traditional French dish. This version is an easy one-pot meal that's ready in just 25 minutes. It makes for the perfect hearty appetizer (especially when paired with a substantial salad, like it is here), or it can be combined with pasta for a hearty entrée. Don't forget the crusty bread, which is perfect for soaking up every last bit of the savory white wine and garlic sauce.

**2 pounds live mussels**

**1 cup dry white wine**

**3 garlic cloves, minced**

**1 tablespoon minced white onion**

**Sea salt**

**Freshly ground black pepper**

**3 tablespoons unsalted butter**

**2 tablespoons chopped fresh parsley**

**1 teaspoon dried basil**

**½ baguette, French bread loaf, or other crusty bread loaf, sliced**

1. Put the mussels in a colander and rinse them under cold water, gently shaking to ensure all are clean. Using a small, sharp knife, carefully scrape any dirt and beards (strings) off the shells.

2. Using your fingernail, tap any mussel that is already open. If it doesn't close when you tap it, discard it.

3. In a large pot over medium heat, combine the wine, garlic, and onion and season with salt and pepper. Bring to a simmer and cook for 5 minutes.

4. Carefully add the mussels to the pot, cover, and turn the heat to high. Cook for 5 minutes.

5. Stir in the butter, parsley, and basil and remove the pan from the heat. Remove and discard any mussels that haven't opened during the cooking process.

CONTINUED >>

**Mussels in White Wine and Garlic with Crusty Bread** CONTINUED

6. Divide the mussels and broth evenly between two bowls and serve with the sliced bread.

**TIP:** This is one of those meals that strikes a great balance between seeming like something you'd find at a fancy restaurant and being simple and quick to make. You can easily double or triple this recipe to impress friends and family who come over for dinner any night of the week—just make sure you have a big enough pot. Practice while it's just the two of you, then branch out to make dinner for a group when you feel like inviting another couple or two over.

**FOR THE SOUS-CHEF:** Clean the mussels in steps 1 and 2 while the chef preps for step 3 by mincing the garlic and onion. While the chef is working on the wine broth in step 3, chop the parsley.

# Roasted Chickpea and Green Bean Salad

**SERVES 2** ♥ **PREP TIME:** 10 MINUTES ♥ **COOK TIME:** 25 MINUTES

**VEGAN**

When I think of Paris, I first think about heavier foods like bread, butter, and cream sauces. But there's a lighter side to the city's food culture to consider, too. This dish is the perfect reminder. Ripe, juicy tomatoes tossed with olive oil, lemon juice, and fresh herbs make for a salad that can't be beat—until it's topped with roasted chickpeas and green beans. The roasting process intensifies the flavors and adds crunch to this delectable duo.

- 1 cup green beans, ends trimmed
- 2 cups canned chickpeas, rinsed and drained
- 3 tablespoons extra-virgin olive oil, divided
- Salt
- Freshly ground black pepper
- 2 large tomatoes, quartered
- 1 tablespoon chopped fresh parsley
- 1 tablespoon chopped fresh basil
- 1 teaspoon smoked paprika
- 2 tablespoons freshly squeezed lemon juice

1. Preheat the oven to 400°F.

2. In a medium bowl, toss the green beans and chickpeas with 2 tablespoons of olive oil and season with salt and pepper. Spread them out on a baking sheet and bake for 25 minutes, stirring occasionally, or until the chickpeas are crisp and the green beans are tender and lightly browned.

3. In a large bowl, mix together the tomatoes, parsley, basil, remaining 1 tablespoon of olive oil, the paprika, and lemon juice. Season generously with salt and pepper. Divide the mixture between two plates, top each with half of the roasted chickpea and green bean mixture, and serve immediately.

**FOR THE SOUS-CHEF:** While the chef preheats the oven and opens, drains, and rinses the chickpeas, trim the ends off the green beans. Later, chop the herbs and quarter the tomatoes while the chef measures the ingredients and takes the chickpeas and beans out of the oven.

# Coffee Crème Brûlée

**SERVES 2 ♥ PREP TIME:** 10 MINUTES ♥ **COOK TIME:** 1 HOUR 10 MINUTES, PLUS 30 MINUTES TO CHILL

**5-INGREDIENT, VEGETARIAN**

When I go out and crème brûlée is on the menu, there's no question about what I'm ordering. And while I used to think it was too intimidating to make at home, it's actually not that hard. Using the oven's broiler, you can easily replicate the classic technique and make this restaurant-style dessert at home. There are several steps and a lot of waiting, so make this recipe in advance if you can.

2 large egg yolks
8 tablespoons sugar, divided
¾ cup heavy (whipping) cream

1½ teaspoons instant coffee
¼ teaspoon vanilla extract

1. Preheat the oven to 300°F.

2. In a medium bowl, whisk the egg yolks and 3 tablespoons of sugar for 1 minute. Set aside.

3. In a separate bowl, whisk half of the heavy cream with the coffee until the mixture is smooth and the coffee has dissolved. Add the remaining 5 tablespoons of heavy cream and whisk until fully combined.

4. Carefully pour the coffee mixture into the egg yolk mixture and gently fold together.

5. Divide the crème brûlée mixture between two ramekins, being sure not to fill them all the way to the top.

6. Place the ramekins into an oven-safe dish that is slightly larger and has taller sides than the ramekins.

7. Put the dish in the oven. Carefully pour water into the dish to surround the ramekins until the water reaches halfway up the sides.

8. Bake for 45 to 60 minutes and remove the dish when the middle is no longer liquid. (You do want it jiggly, though!)

9. Remove the ramekins from the water and allow them to cool, then refrigerate them for about 30 minutes (more is fine).

10. Sprinkle the remaining 5 tablespoons of sugar over the tops of the crème brûlées in a thin layer, then broil for 5 to 10 minutes, until golden brown on top.

11. Serve warm or refrigerate for a few minutes again so they can be served cold.

**TIP:** If you happen to have a kitchen torch, you can use that instead of the broiler to caramelize the sugar on top.

**FOR THE SOUS-CHEF:** Preheat the oven, then whisk the egg yolks and sugar while the chef whisks the ingredients in step 3.

# ACTIVITY: Design a National Birthday Bash

Your birthday is declared a national holiday! How should people around the country celebrate?

Have you ever thought about your perfect birthday party? One where everyone—yes, everyone—is forced to take a day off work and celebrate it? Well, tonight is your chance to imagine it and design it, so that you are prepared in the event that the wider world suddenly recognizes what your partner already does—you should be celebrated and in a BIG way! Don't worry, there's no pressure to perfect your party for tonight's dinner. This is something you can work on together while you enjoy tonight's delicious meal. Then why not give your birthday week a national holiday test run where you refine the details by test-celebrating them?

**Supplies needed:** Pen and paper (optional)

**Estimated time:** 20+ minutes (and a week to test)

## INSTRUCTIONS

Sit down with a pen, paper, and your significant other, and use the following questions to decide what the national celebrations would look like.

1. What are the qualities about you that people would be celebrating?
2. What are your favorite ways of celebrating: Cookouts? Fireworks? Parades? An all-night dance party? A quiet retreat in the woods?
3. What's the symbol of the day: A bottle of champagne? A sparkler? A bird or animal? A food?
4. What are the decoration colors that best reflect your personality?
5. What music should be played? What food should be served? What movie should be on 24-hour repeat?
6. What one special thing would you do just for yourself?

# BIG NEWS, BIG FLAVORS

If you're craving intense flavors, you'll love this menu with its sweet and spicy salmon, simple salad with tangy red wine dressing and fresh garlic, refreshing limeade with a kick, and corn bread muffins. This menu is perfect for when you have something to celebrate that isn't a holiday or birthday (though you could certainly use it for those, too), like a new job, engagement, or accomplishment. It's good for any time of year because there's such a range of flavors to savor along with your good news. Congrats, by the way!

## MENU

*Honey Sriracha–
Glazed Salmon*

*Zesty Romaine Salad*

*Corn Bread Muffins*

*Ginger Limeade*

## CHEERS!

The ginger limeade in this menu is delicious as is, but you can also turn it into a cocktail by adding a shot of vodka. A bold white wine, like a Chardonnay or dry Riesling, would also pair well with these strong flavors.

# Honey Sriracha–Glazed Salmon

**SERVES 2** ♥ **PREP TIME:** 5 MINUTES, PLUS 1 HOUR TO MARINATE ♥ **COOK TIME:** 15 MINUTES

We love salmon for its versatility: You can panfry it to get a nice crispness, grill it in the summertime, or even steam it. This version packs a punch by combining fiery sriracha with salty soy sauce and supersweet honey—it's the best of all taste worlds combined! Baking it is my favorite part because it doesn't need my attention once it's in the oven. And because you bake it right on parchment paper, cleanup couldn't be easier.

**2 (4-ounce) salmon fillets**
**2 tablespoons soy sauce**
**1 tablespoon honey**

**1½ teaspoons rice vinegar**
**1½ teaspoons sriracha**
**1 garlic clove, minced**

1. Place the salmon fillets on a rimmed baking dish.

2. In a medium bowl, whisk the soy sauce, honey, rice vinegar, sriracha, and garlic. Pour the mixture over the salmon so the fillets are evenly coated. Refrigerate for 1 hour, turning the salmon once.

3. Preheat the oven to 425°F. Line a baking sheet with parchment paper.

4. Transfer the salmon to the baking sheet and bake for 12 to 14 minutes, until the salmon is flaky.

**TIP:** If you know you're not going to have a ton of time to marinate the salmon when you get home from work, build the marinade in the morning and let the fish rest in it for up to 8 hours before cooking.

**FOR THE SOUS-CHEF:** Preheat the oven and prep the sauce.

# Zesty Romaine Salad

**SERVES 2 ♥ PREP TIME:** 5 MINUTES

30-MINUTE, ONE-POT, VEGETARIAN

Every cook needs a go-to salad to use as a side dish that'll go with just about anything. This one is a mix of crunchy greens tossed in a punchy red wine vinegar dressing with fresh garlic and dried herbs. Make the dressing ahead of time and keep it in the refrigerator, or wait until it's time to make the salad and make it right there in the bottom of the bowl (it makes cleanup easy).

**5 teaspoons extra-virgin olive oil**
**1 tablespoon red wine vinegar**
**1 teaspoons Dijon mustard**
**¼ teaspoon dried oregano**
**Kosher salt**
**1 small garlic clove**

**1 romaine heart, cut crosswise into 1-inch ribbons**
**1 medium tomato, diced**
**¼ red onion, diced**
**Shaved Parmesan cheese, for garnish (optional)**

1. In a medium bowl, combine the olive oil, vinegar, mustard, oregano, and salt to taste. Using a zester or the zesting side of a box grater, finely grate the garlic directly into the bowl. Whisk the dressing until it has emulsified.

2. Add the romaine, tomato, and onion and toss everything with the dressing. Garnish with Parmesan (if using) and serve.

**TIP:** If you want even more flavor, you can add some bacon and make your own bacon-flavored croutons. Remove the crusts from a slice of hearty sourdough or white bread and cut it into large cubes. In a small pan over medium-high heat, cook 2 slices of bacon, flipping as necessary, until crisp, about 5 minutes. Remove the bacon and set it aside. Put the bread cubes into the pan and cook, flipping, until the cubes are brown on three or four sides. Add the crumbled bacon and croutons to the salad in step 2, along with the cheese (if using).

**FOR THE SOUS-CHEF:** Cut up the vegetables while the chef prepares the dressing.

# Corn Bread Muffins

**MAKES 12 MUFFINS** ♥ **PREP TIME:** 10 MINUTES ♥ **COOK TIME:** 20 MINUTES

30-MINUTE, VEGETARIAN

I'm from the South, so I grew up eating all kinds of corn bread. My favorite way to enjoy it, though, is in muffin form. It makes it easy to grab just enough for one or two people and store the rest for later (plus, it's just fun to eat that way). You could also use this recipe with a loaf pan if you don't have a muffin tin.

| | |
|---|---|
| 1 cup all-purpose flour | ½ teaspoon sea salt |
| 1 cup cornmeal | 1 cup whole milk |
| ⅓ cup sugar | 1 egg, beaten |
| 2 teaspoons baking powder | ¼ cup vegetable oil |

1. Preheat the oven to 400°F. Line a muffin tin with paper liners and set aside.

2. In a large bowl, stir together the flour, cornmeal, sugar, baking powder, and salt. Add the milk, egg, and vegetable oil and stir to combine.

3. Spoon the batter into the prepared muffin cups. Bake for 15 to 20 minutes or until the muffins are golden brown and a toothpick inserted into the center of one comes out clean.

**TIP:** To give the corn bread even more flavor, stir in a spoonful of canned chopped green chiles. You can find a wide variety, from very mild to nice and spicy!

**FOR THE SOUS-CHEF:** Preheat the oven and line the muffin tin while the chef prepares the batter. Once the batter is complete, help the chef spoon the batter into the muffin cups.

# Ginger Limeade

**SERVES 1 ♥ PREP TIME:** 5 MINUTES, PLUS 40 MINUTES TO MAKE THE GINGER SYRUP

5-INGREDIENT, 30-MINUTE, VEGAN

Once you try this drink for date night, you may decide you want to have a pitcher of this slightly spicy yet fabulously refreshing beverage in the refrigerator all summer. It's alcohol-free, so you can enjoy it any time of day. For a stronger ginger flavor, use ½ cup of chopped ginger. If you like the ginger flavor to stay in the background, just use ¼ cup.

## FOR THE GINGER SYRUP

1 cup water

1 cup sugar

¼ to ½ cup peeled and chopped fresh ginger

## FOR THE DRINK

1 ounce freshly squeezed lime juice

1 ounce ginger syrup

4 ounces cold water

Lime slice, for garnish

1. **To make the ginger syrup:** In a small saucepan over medium heat, combine the water and sugar, stirring frequently, until the sugar has dissolved. Add the ginger and bring to a boil.

2. Reduce the heat to low and simmer for 10 minutes. Remove from the heat and allow to cool fully before straining out the ginger.

3. **To make the drink:** Combine the lime juice, ginger syrup, and water in a cocktail shaker. Fill three-quarters of the shaker with ice cubes and shake for about 12 seconds, or until chilled.

4. Fill a highball glass with ice. Strain the drink into the glass and garnish with a lime slice.

**TIP:** If you prefer a sparkling limeade, shake the lime juice, syrup, and 1 ounce of water until chilled. Strain into the ice-filled glass, then top with 3 ounces of soda water.

**FOR THE SOUS-CHEF:** This recipe makes just one drink at a time, so each of you can make your own.

## ACTIVITY: **Never Have I Ever**

You'll be surprised by what you learn about your partner in this game. Get to know each other better and see how well you *already* know each other with this exchange. Hilarity can ensue, so enjoy being silly. Get creative here and use it as a way to share some of your funniest or most embarrassing experiences. If you want, you can specify a theme related to your big news ("Never have I ever replied all to a work email.") Or use the prompts below to get you started.

**Supplies needed:** 4 paper plates (optional)
Pen or marker (optional)
4 ice-pop sticks or similar (optional)
Tape or glue (optional)

**Estimated time:** 10 minutes or as long as you want to play

### INSTRUCTIONS

1.  You could play with verbal responses, but if you'd prefer to have signs, start by prepping your materials. Write "I haven't!" on two plates and "I have!" on the other two. Tape or glue an ice-pop stick to the back of each plate to use as handles.

2.  Start off with, "I've never . . ." and say something you've never done. The other person then holds up a plate that says they either have or haven't done the thing you named. Take turns naming things you've never done.

3.  Feel free to take control and come up with your own situations (stay away from anything that might spark an argument, of course!), but here are a few to get you started:

    ▶ Rolled down a hill

    ▶ Eaten squid

    ▶ Fallen on my face in public

- ▶ Gone to a concert

- ▶ Peeked at Christmas presents

- ▶ Gotten a pedicure

- ▶ Purchased something from an infomercial

- ▶ Fed a giraffe

- ▶ Entered a talent show

- ▶ Met a celebrity

- ▶ Been on the radio/television

- ▶ Gone skinny-dipping

- ▶ Learned to roller-skate

**4.** If you do want a way to keep score and win the game, keep a tally of how many things each of you has done that the other one has not. The first one to 10 wins.

**TIP:** Instead of repeating the phrase "Never have I ever," you can just name an action (whether you've done it or not) and simultaneously hold up your plates to see who has or has not done that thing.

*Mango Salsa Pork Chops,*
**PAGE 97**

# Staycations

I love visiting new places and trying new things, but it's not always feasible to pack our bags, hop on a plane, and go somewhere new and exciting. What you *can* do is sample a new place with your taste buds. It's the cheapest and least stressful way to go wherever you want, with very little planning.

# VIVA ITALIA

Dreaming of taking a luxurious Italian vacation together? If it's not a good time for an impromptu European vacation, the next best thing is this menu, which boasts Zuppa di Pesce (a dish that's popular along the Tuscan coast of Italy), a classic fresh caprese salad, and sweet chocolate-hazelnut semifreddo. It's a quintessential romantic meal. I like this one because it's Italian dinner, but there's no spaghetti or lasagna in sight. Be sure you get a head start making the dessert so it'll be ready by the time you're done with the main course.

## MENU

*Chopped Caprese Salad
with Balsamic Vinegar*

*Zuppa di Pesce*

*Stracciatella Semifreddo*

## CHEERS!

If you feel up to it, try making a traditional Italian drink: the Negroni. Stir together equal parts (1 ounce each) gin, vermouth rosso, and Campari, and pour over ice. Perch a slice of orange on the rim of the glass.

# Chopped Caprese Salad with Balsamic Vinegar

**SERVES 2 ♥ PREP TIME:** 10 MINUTES

30-MINUTE, ONE POT, VEGETARIAN

*Caprese* refers to Capri, that tiny, tall, beautiful island surrounded by the shimmering sea off the Amalfi Coast in the Italian region of Campania. This version is easier to eat than the traditional recipe (with ingredients sliced and stacked up) because everything's cut into bite-size chunks. Choose the freshest ingredients possible for the most flavor—I love heirloom tomatoes in this. Instead of balsamic vinegar and olive oil, you could try bottled balsamic glaze for a sweeter but still tangy take.

- **2 or 3 ripe tomatoes, cut into bite-size chunks**
- **¾ cup small mozzarella balls (bocconcini), halved**
- **½ shallot, minced**
- **2 or 3 sprigs basil leaves, torn into bite-size pieces**
- **2 or 3 sprigs mint leaves, torn into bite-size pieces**
- **½ teaspoon dried oregano**
- **2 tablespoons extra-virgin olive oil**
- **1½ tablespoons balsamic vinegar**
- **Salt**
- **Freshly ground black pepper**

1. In a medium mixing bowl, combine the tomatoes, mozzarella, shallot, basil, mint, and oregano. Toss well.

2. Drizzle with the olive oil and balsamic vinegar, season with salt and pepper, and toss to coat. Serve.

**SWAP:** If you can't find the bocconcini, cut up a larger fresh mozzarella ball into bite-size pieces.

**FOR THE SOUS-CHEF:** Peel and mince the shallot; if you finish before your partner (who's cutting tomatoes and mozzarella balls), go ahead and tear the basil and mint leaves.

# Zuppa di Pesce

**SERVES 2 ♥ PREP TIME:** 15 MINUTES ♥ **COOK TIME:** 20 MINUTES

ONE POT

*Zuppa di pesce* means "fish soup," which may not sound like such a delicious meal at all, much less a date night one. Don't let the name put you off, though. This is a simple, wholesome dish best enjoyed while you are curled up with your special someone, in pajamas, in front of your favorite show. You can enjoy it during any season.

2 cups water

1 cup seafood stock

1 tablespoon Old Bay seasoning

Salt

1 medium red potato, quartered

1 ear corn, cut into 4 pieces

1 pound jumbo tail-on shrimp, deveined

4 ounces sea scallops

½ teaspoon red pepper flakes (optional)

1 tablespoon chopped fresh parsley (optional)

1. In a Dutch oven, bring the water, stock, Old Bay seasoning, and salt to taste to a boil.

2. Stir in the potato and corn and cook for 8 to 10 minutes, or until the potato is tender.

3. Add the shrimp and scallops and cook for 3 to 4 minutes, until cooked through.

4. Sprinkle with red pepper flakes (if using) and parsley (if using) before serving.

**TIP:** Include any sturdy fish or shellfish you wish in this stew, such as mussels, clams, or cod.

**FOR THE SOUS-CHEF:** This recipe is really a job for one person, so once you've helped chop everything up, move on to the pistachio mixture in the next recipe or pour some wine for the two of you.

# Stracciatella Semifreddo

**SERVES 2 ♥ PREP TIME:** 10 MINUTES, PLUS 1 HOUR TO FREEZE

**VEGETARIAN**

If you have never tried a semifreddo, the classic Italian dessert, you are in for a treat! *Semifreddo* means "half-cold" or "half-frozen," and its texture is somewhere between a frozen mousse and gelato. In other words, it's creamy, decadent, and something you are going to love. In this version, chocolate-hazelnut spread is woven throughout, and chocolate chips add texture. You can also add your own twist by swapping in whatever toppings and mix-ins you choose. Try fruit, nuts, or your favorite candies.

¼ cup plus 2 tablespoons heavy (whipping) cream, divided

1 tablespoon powdered sugar

1 teaspoon vanilla extract

8 tablespoons cream cheese, at room temperature

2 tablespoons chocolate-hazelnut spread

2 tablespoons semisweet chocolate chips

1. In a medium bowl, combine ¼ cup of heavy cream, the powdered sugar, and vanilla. Using a handheld electric mixer or a stand mixer, beat on high speed until peaks form. Set aside.

2. In a separate bowl, with clean beaters, mix together the cream cheese and remaining 2 tablespoons of heavy cream for 1 minute. Add the chocolate-hazelnut spread and chocolate chips. Using a spatula, evenly distribute the chips through-out the mixture.

3. Using a spatula, fold the whipped cream mixture into the cream cheese mixture. Pour into two small dishes, cover with aluminum foil or plastic wrap, and freeze for 1 hour before serving.

**FOR THE SOUS-CHEF:** If you have an extra mixer, jump ahead to step 2 to make the cream-cheese mixture while the chef is working on the whipped cream mixture in step 1.

## ACTIVITY: I Can Show You the World

If you and/or your partner haven't traveled the world much, feel free to limit this to the states instead. If you have had the opportunity to travel (lucky you!), you'll love this one. In this exercise, each partner will write down which countries they've visited.

**Supplies needed:** Pen or pencil and paper

### INSTRUCTIONS

Use the following prompts to discuss your visits and decide where you'd like to go together.

- ▶ My favorite country was . . .

- ▶ The weather was . . .

- ▶ I loved it because . . .

- ▶ The most interesting food I ate there was . . .

- ▶ If we go here together, we absolutely have to visit (person, tourist attraction, etc.) . . .

- ▶ The people were . . .

- ▶ The energy/vibe was . . .

- ▶ My best memory from this country was . . .

Don't stop there! Keep sharing about your adventures.

# TROPICAL PARADISE

If your idea of the perfect getaway is more beach than mountains, you're going to love this date. Search online for a video that plays ocean sounds and scenes for hours to set the mood. Put on the outfits you'd wear for a night out if you were really at the beach, then enjoy your spicy, fruity foods and mai tais without the hefty hotel and airline fees. While you're relaxing, plan your next trip. This date is the next best thing to having your feet in the sand and a breeze in your hair.

## MENU

*Chili-Lime Shrimp Salad*
*Mango Salsa Pork Chops*
*Mai Tai*

## CHEERS!

If mai tais aren't your thing, try a sweet white wine. If you'd rather not have alcohol, you'll love iced tea or even fruit-infused water with this menu. To make some, start the day before, and leave cut fruit in water in the refrigerator to steep for 12 to 24 hours. Mango-strawberry water would be delicious here.

# Chili-Lime Shrimp Salad

**SERVES 2 ♥ PREP TIME:** 15 MINUTES ♥ **COOK TIME:** 5 MINUTES

30-MINUTE

Let's spice things up this evening! For such a simple salad, this really packs a lot of flavor. The chili-lime vinaigrette is so satisfyingly lip-smacking, tangy, and sweet. You can omit the shrimp if it is not your thing—lump crab, salmon, or pulled chicken would also be delightful.

## FOR THE SALAD

2 heads hearts of romaine lettuce, chopped

1 cup cherry tomatoes, halved

1 avocado, pitted and sliced

½ bunch fresh cilantro, stemmed

16 shrimp, shelled

1 tablespoon butter

Chili powder

Salt

## FOR THE DRESSING

Juice of 1 lime

2 teaspoons honey

1 tablespoon extra-virgin olive oil

¼ teaspoon chili powder, plus more as needed

¼ teaspoon salt, plus more as needed

1. **To make the salad:** In a large serving bowl, combine the romaine lettuce, tomatoes, avocado, and cilantro.

2. Pat the shrimp dry with paper towels. In a large skillet, melt the butter over medium-high heat. Add the shrimp and sprinkle with chili powder and salt to taste. Cook for 1 to 2 minutes, then flip and cook for 1 to 2 minutes more, or until the shrimp just become opaque. Remove from the heat. Let cool slightly. Add the shrimp to the salad.

3. **To make the dressing:** In a small mixing bowl, whisk together the lime juice, honey, olive oil, chili powder, and salt. Drizzle the vinaigrette over the salad and toss. Adjust the seasoning to taste by adding more chili powder or salt.

**FOR THE SOUS-CHEF:** While the chef assembles the salad ingredients and cooks the shrimp, prepare the dressing.

# Mango Salsa Pork Chops

**SERVES 2 ♥ PREP TIME:** 10 MINUTES ♥ **COOK TIME:** 15 MINUTES
**30-MINUTE**

Pork chops cook up quickly in a skillet and don't need much seasoning when topped with a tasty salsa. If you're short on time, you can use store-bought salsa. Since it's date night, and two of you can work on it together, though, I recommend taking the time to make this mango one. It's not hard to throw together (you cook it right in the same skillet you'll use for the meat), and the tropical flavors will bring out the sweetness in the pork and marry perfectly with the flavors of the shrimp salad and the mai tais.

½ cup quick-cooking white or brown rice or microwavable pouch rice

1 teaspoon avocado oil, plus 1 tablespoon

2 to 4 tablespoons minced jalapeño pepper

¾ cup diced mango (about 1 mango)

3 tablespoons diced red onion

Juice of ½ lime

2 lean boneless pork loin chops (½ to ¾ inch thick)

Kosher salt

Freshly ground black pepper

1 (8-ounce) bag sugar snap peas

1 tablespoon minced fresh cilantro (optional)

1. Prepare the rice according to the package instructions.

2. In a medium skillet, heat 1 teaspoon of oil over medium-high heat until it shimmers. Add the jalapeño pepper and cook for about 2 minutes, until softened. Transfer to a bowl. Add the mango, onion, and lime juice. Stir to combine.

3. Season the pork chops on both sides with a pinch each of salt and black pepper.

CONTINUED >>

**Mango Salsa Pork Chops** CONTINUED

4. In the same skillet you used for the salsa, heat the remaining 1 tablespoon of oil until it shimmers. Add the pork chops and cook for about 4 minutes on each side, until the internal temperature reaches a minimum of 145°F. Remove from the heat.

5. Meanwhile, cook the snap peas according to the package instructions.

6. Divide the snap peas evenly between two plates. Stir the cilantro (if using) into the cooked rice and divide the rice evenly alongside the sugar snap peas. Plate the pork chops and top with the mango salsa.

**FOR THE SOUS-CHEF:** Microwave the rice and make the salsa while the chef cooks the pork chops. Cook the sugar snap peas while or after the rice cooks, depending on the directions on the bag. Still have time on your hands? Move on to the mai tais.

# Mai Tai

**SERVES 2 ♥ PREP TIME:** 5 MINUTES

5-INGREDIENT, 30-MINUTE, VEGAN

The mai tai is one of the most famous tropical, or "tiki"-style, cocktails. The origin of the cocktail's name is said to be the Tahitian word *maita'i*, meaning "good." I have to agree. Nothing related to a beach vacation could ever be labeled as anything other than good, right? The fresh flavors in the mai tai effortlessly complement the seafood, fruit, and spiciness of the meal.

4 ounces aged rum
1½ ounces freshly squeezed
  lime juice

1 ounce triple sec
½ ounce orgeat
Mint sprigs, for garnish

1. In a cocktail shaker, combine the rum, lime juice, triple sec, and orgeat.

2. Whip-shake the cocktail by adding a few ice cubes and shaking until the cubes dissolve.

3. Fill rocks glasses with crushed ice.

4. Pour the cocktail into the glasses and garnish with a sprig of mint.

**SWAP:** If you can't find orgeat, which is a syrup with a nutty-floral flavor, you can use almond syrup instead. Amaretto syrup could also work.

**FOR THE SOUS-CHEF:** You can whip these up while the chef works on the pork chops.

## ACTIVITY: Plan Your Dream Vacation

Have a relaxing evening by taking some time to fantasize about your perfect getaway with your partner. Don't let the thought of the expense limit you—just imagine whisking each other away to new places. You could visit a tropical island and tour Europe in the same night. Let yourself get carried away by your wildest travel dreams.

**Supplies needed:** Pen or pencil (optional)
Paper (optional)
Internet connection
Candles (optional)
A device to play background sounds (optional)

**Estimated time:** 30 minutes to 1 hour

### INSTRUCTIONS

1. Brainstorm and create an itinerary. Imagine what you'll see (doodle it on your itinerary!), how you'll feel, what the weather will be like, what you'll eat, what you'll wear, and what you'll shop for.

2. Set the mood with scented candles, if you have any that fit the vibe of the vacation you're planning. Play some of the sounds you'd hear if you were there, like waves crashing against the shore, the ambient sounds of a coffee shop, or forest sounds.

3. Close your eyes and walk through your trip together, keeping the itinerary handy to guide you through your imaginary getaway. Save it in case you need ideas for the real thing later.

**TIP:** Use Google Earth to virtually visit the places on your list.

# CALIFORNIA COAST

Since I was a child, I've dreamed of visiting the California coast to soak up the sunshine, enjoy the ocean sounds, and experience the overall vibe. We've yet to make the cross-country road trip, but that doesn't mean I can't take inspiration from my dream and put together a menu that meshes the health-conscious foods and levels of relaxation I imagine I'd find there. Here, the zucchini soup sets the stage, the pistachio-crusted halibut pays homage to both the state's coastal waters and its agricultural bounty, and you get to wash it all down with a refreshing margarita. It's a summer vacation in an evening.

## MENU

*Cream of Zucchini Soup with Cumin and Coriander*

*Pistachio-Crusted Halibut*

*Tommy's Margarita*

## CHEERS!

Enjoy a dry white wine if you'd rather not make the margaritas. Try a California Chardonnay, pinot gris, or sauvignon blanc. If you prefer reds, like I do, try a Central Coast Pinot Noir, but nothing too full-bodied. You could also make virgin margaritas by trading tequila for sparkling water (use extra, and choose from lemon, lime, or plain), as well as a splash of orange juice.

# Cream of Zucchini Soup with Cumin and Coriander

**SERVES 2 ♥ PREP TIME:** 10 MINUTES ♥ **COOK TIME:** 20 MINUTES

30-MINUTE, ONE POT, VEGETARIAN

I grew up eating zucchini in sliced form, sautéed on the stove or grilled. For the longest time, that was the only way I ever made it, usually with a little garlic, onion, pepper, and salt. Then I discovered zucchini soup. This recipe is a deliciously simple one-pot cream of zucchini soup that is creamy, bright, and a little earthy all at the same time. Feel free to double the recipe so you have enough for leftovers.

| | |
|---|---|
| 1 tablespoon butter | 1 cup heavy (whipping) cream |
| 1 garlic clove, chopped | ½ teaspoon salt |
| ¼ yellow onion, chopped | Pinch ground cumin |
| 2 zucchini, chopped | Pinch ground coriander |
| 1 cup vegetable stock | Freshly ground black pepper |

1. In a medium stockpot, melt the butter over medium heat. Add the garlic and onion. Sauté for about 5 minutes, or until translucent.

2. Add the zucchini and stock. Simmer for about 5 minutes, or until the zucchini is soft.

3. Use an immersion blender, or let cool slightly and pour into a countertop blender. Blend until smooth. (If using a standing blender, return the soup to the pot.)

4. Add the heavy cream, salt, cumin, coriander, and pepper. Simmer over medium-low heat for about 10 minutes. Remove from the heat.

**FOR THE SOUS-CHEF:** Once everything's chopped, this dish requires only one person's attention. That puts you in charge of making the drinks while your partner manages the soup.

# Pistachio-Crusted Halibut

**SERVES 2 ♥ PREP TIME:** 10 MINUTES ♥ **COOK TIME:** 15 MINUTES

30-MINUTE

If you want an impressive dish that isn't difficult to prepare, look no further. This pistachio-crusted halibut is easy enough for a beginner to cook but fancy and tasty enough for a date night at home. This dish also pairs well with potatoes and roasted vegetables. Depending on which ones you decide to cook, you can throw those in the oven when you start the Cream of Zucchini Soup with Cumin and Coriander or the halibut.

**Nonstick cooking spray**
**¼ cup shelled unsalted pistachios**
**2 tablespoons unseasoned bread crumbs**
**1 garlic clove, minced**

**1 tablespoon butter, melted**
**¼ teaspoon salt**
**2 (6-ounce) halibut fillets**
**1 tablespoon Dijon mustard**

1. Preheat the oven to 400°F. Spray a small baking dish with nonstick cooking spray.

2. In a food processor, combine the pistachios, bread crumbs, garlic, butter, and salt. Pulse until it resembles coarse crumbs.

3. Place the halibut fillets in the baking dish and spread the mustard over them. Press the pistachio mixture on top.

4. Bake the halibut for 10 to 12 minutes, until it flakes easily. Serve and enjoy.

**TIP:** If you use salted pistachios, adjust the amount of salt listed in the ingredients accordingly.

**SWAP:** I like to use halibut to make this dish, but I've also tried tilapia and cod with equally delicious results.

**FOR THE SOUS-CHEF:** Make the pistachio topping while the chef prepares the halibut.

# Tommy's Margarita

**SERVES 2** ♥ **PREP TIME:** 5 MINUTES

5-INGREDIENT, 30-MINUTE, VEGAN

Tommy's Margarita is a popular variation on the classic that uses agave syrup in place of orange liqueur. It was invented in the 1990s by Julio Bermejo at Tommy's Mexican Restaurant in San Francisco, California. Bermejo's margarita variation was unique at the time for its use of agave syrup and 100 percent blue agave tequila. Tequilas made with less than 51 percent blue agave, or tequila "mixto," were less expensive and more commonly used in cocktails at the time.

**4 ounces 100 percent blue agave tequila**

**2 ounces freshly squeezed lime juice**

**1 ounce agave syrup**

**Lime wedges, for garnish**

1. Pour the tequila, lime juice, and syrup into a cocktail shaker.

2. Fill three-quarters of the shaker with ice.

3. Shake until chilled, about 12 seconds.

4. Strain the drink into two rocks glasses filled with ice and garnish with a lime wedge.

**FOR THE SOUS-CHEF:** You'll probably be working on these while your partner oversees the pot of soup, but if the two of you are working on the drinks, one person can gather the ingredients while the other measures and pours.

## ACTIVITY: What a Trip

What is the first trip you remember taking as a kid? Share all the details you remember with each other so your significant other can get a true glimpse of your childhood.

# SCANDINAVIAN SUMMER

Bright flavors are my favorite things about a meal plan inspired by a Scandinavian summer. I'm a sucker for dill and lemon, and this combination of eggs Benedict with fresh greens, bright cucumber noodles, and crispy vegetable fritters is wonderfully bright and fresh. Since Scandinavian summers are full of almost endless sunshine, embrace that feeling by arranging this meal somewhere sunny, whether it's by a window or at a nice brunch spot outside.

## MENU

*Norwegian Eggs Benedict*

*Dill Cucumber Noodles*

*Carrot and Leek Fritters with Dill Dipping Sauce*

## CHEERS!

If you really want to go all in on the theme, pick up a bottle of akvavit (aquavit), chill it, and sip it alongside your meal or use it in a cocktail (like akvavit and tonic). You could also enjoy a pale ale or a mimosa (half sparkling wine, half orange juice). If you have access to a certain iconic Scandinavian furniture store (or, more specifically, their food section), you could even pick up a non-alcoholic lingonberry soda.

# Norwegian Eggs Benedict

**SERVES 2** ♥ **PREP TIME:** 10 MINUTES ♥ **COOK TIME:** 10 MINUTES

30-MINUTE

To me, there is nothing more satisfying than the creaminess of a poached egg paired with the saltiness of smoked salmon and capers. Add that to a thick slice of bread with buttery flavor and you've got yourself an especially filling, delicious meal. This hearty brunch recipe can be enjoyed anytime—what's better than breakfast for dinner? If you've never poached eggs, don't let the process scare you. They're actually pretty fun to make.

4 cups water

1 tablespoon white vinegar

2 large eggs

½ cup arugula

4 smoked salmon slices

2 brioche slices, toasted

1 teaspoon capers

Freshly ground black pepper

1. In a medium pot, bring the water to a low simmer. Add the white vinegar, which will help set the eggs more quickly.

2. Gently crack the eggs into a bowl without breaking the yolks. Slowly pour the eggs, one at a time, into the water and simmer until the egg whites turn white, about 2 minutes. Using a slotted spoon, gently remove the eggs from the water and place them on a paper towel–lined plate to drain.

3. Arrange ¼ cup of arugula, 2 slices of smoked salmon, and 1 egg on each slice of toast. Top with ½ teaspoon of capers on each slice and sprinkle with pepper. Serve while the eggs are hot.

**SWAP:** Replace the brioche with bagels, baguette slices, or your favorite toast.

**FOR THE SOUS-CHEF:** While the chef poaches the eggs, arrange the arugula and salmon on the toast.

# Dill Cucumber Noodles

**SERVES 2 ♥ PREP TIME:** 10 MINUTES

30-MINUTE, VEGETARIAN

If you have a spiralizer, you may know your way around zucchini "noodles," but why not try on cucumber for a crunchy change? This salad will not keep very well due to the water content of the cucumber—the salt will cause it to leach liquid as the dish sits—so "zoodle" only as much cucumber as you would like to eat in one sitting.

2 large cucumbers

2 teaspoons freshly squeezed lemon juice

1 teaspoon Dijon mustard

2 tablespoons minced red onion

1 tablespoon extra-virgin olive oil

¼ teaspoon salt

2 tablespoons sour cream

1 tablespoon chopped fresh dill

1 tablespoon capers (optional)

Freshly ground black pepper

1. Spiralize the cucumbers into a medium mixing bowl. (If you do not have a spiralizer to make the cucumber noodles, use a vegetable peeler to peel long ribbons out of the skin and flesh of the cucumber until you get to the seedy center. Discard the seeds.)

2. In a small mixing bowl, whisk together the lemon juice, mustard, and onion while drizzling in the olive oil. Add the salt and whisk again. Pour the dressing over the noodles and toss until well coated.

3. Top the noodles with the sour cream, dill, and capers (if using). Serve with several turns of pepper.

**TIP:** If you love red onion, feel free to add some to this recipe. If you have a mandoline, you can use it to make paper-thin slices of onion, which are perfect for not only this dish but also any dish that includes raw onion.

**FOR THE SOUS-CHEF:** While the chef spiralizes the cucumbers, mix the dressing.

# Carrot and Leek Fritters with Dill Dipping Sauce

**SERVES 2** ♥ **PREP TIME:** 10 MINUTES ♥ **COOK TIME:** 20 MINUTES

30-MINUTE, VEGETARIAN

Fritters are a great way to get a serving of vegetables. They're so crunchy and tasty, you might forget you're eating a big pile of spring vegetables. The yogurt-dill dipping sauce complements them perfectly. Serve the fritters warm. They'll balance out the cool, crisp cucumber noodle dish while the yogurt sauce ties the flavors together.

1 large leek, sliced and finely chopped

3 or 4 large carrots, shredded (about 4 cups)

¼ cup all-purpose or whole-wheat flour

3 large eggs, whisked

½ cup crumbled goat cheese

¼ teaspoon salt, plus more for the sauce

Pinch freshly ground black pepper, plus more for the sauce

3 tablespoons extra-virgin olive oil

½ cup plain Greek yogurt

2 tablespoons chopped fresh dill

1. In a medium bowl, combine the leek, carrots, flour, eggs, and goat cheese and stir well. Season with ¼ teaspoon of salt and a pinch of pepper.

2. In a large skillet, heat the olive oil over medium-high heat. Form the carrot and leek mixture into patties, about the same circumference as a ½-cup measuring cup. You should have six fritters total.

3. Place the fritters, two or three at a time, in the large skillet, flattening them with the back of a spatula. Initially, these may seem like they aren't going to stick together, but they will bind up while cooking. Cook for 4 to 5 minutes on each side, until golden brown and warmed through.

**4.** In a medium bowl, mix the yogurt and dill and season with salt and pepper.

**5.** Top the fritters with yogurt sauce. Serve and enjoy.

**SWAP:** You can use sour cream in place of the Greek yogurt and feta cheese instead of goat cheese.

**FOR THE SOUS-CHEF:** Make the yogurt sauce while the chef cooks the fritters.

# ACTIVITY: Scandi Pop Quiz & Prompts

Did you know that couples who travel together have healthier, happier relationships than those who don't? It's true. Studies show that travel helps build and maintain relationships, ignites romance, and leads to higher levels of overall satisfaction. Kick-start your appetite for travel with a food- and Scandinavia-themed quiz. Then use the additional prompts to learn about your travel personalities and travel goals.

**Supplies needed:** Pen and paper (optional to note travel goals)

**Estimated time:** 20 minutes

## QUIZ

Take turns quizzing each other and cover the answers as you go!

1. Which country consumes the most coffee?
2. Who invented the Danish Pastry? Hint: it's known as "Vienna Bread" (*wienerbrød*) in Denmark.
3. Where are Swedish meatballs from?
4. What does the Swedish term *fika* mean?
5. Smalahove is a traditional Norwegian dish of what animal's head?

## QUIZ ANSWERS (COVER THESE WHILE YOU PLAY!)

1. *Finland! The average Finn drinks nearly four cups a day.*
2. *It was first invented by a French baker who later opened a bakery in Italy. Italian bakers took it to Austria, Austrian bakers took it to Denmark, and the rest is jam-filled history.*
3. *Sweden!*
4. *Fika (pronounced FEE-ka) refers to the concept of taking breaks in the day to enjoy coffee or tea, or just to be mindful.*
5. *Sheep! Smalahove is a sheep's head that has been salt-cured, smoked, and steamed. It is served whole with potatoes, beer, and aquavit.*

## PROMPTS

Start out by asking each other the following questions, but add your own to the end, or even in the middle, as the conversation flows.

▶ If you had to choose one place to live, and the decision was to be completely based on the cuisine, where would you move?

▶ What is your true travel personality and has it changed? Would you go backpacking across the world or opt for luxe private resorts? Road less traveled or Instagram hotspots?

▶ Which animal would you travel to see?

▶ What's the most important foreign language phrase to learn?

▶ If there was nothing to hold you back, like money or responsibilities, what would your most luxurious trip look like?

▶ If you could retire anywhere in the world, where would it be and what would you do with your time there?

▶ If we could go on a date anywhere for tonight and be back home tomorrow morning, where would we go and what would we do?

▶ What's something you've recently learned about another country that excites or impresses you?

▶ Where is the weirdest place you have slept?

▶ How many of the Seven Wonders of the World have you seen?

▶ What is your favorite mode of transportation?

# TAKE ME TO MEXICO

One of the cool things about this menu is that you can eat all the dishes with your hands, if you want to. Everything is deceptively simple to make (even the shrimp tacos, which are full of spicy and sweet flavors), so this is even a good option for a weeknight date at home. If it's warm and nice outside, you can take everything to the patio or take a stroll to soak up a little sun before your meal while you chat about your day. Those sweet, spicy shrimp tacos pair well with zesty bean enchiladas and sweet, caramelly mini churros for a well-rounded, fun-to-eat meal.

## MENU

*Shrimp Tacos*
*Bean Empanadas*
*Mini Churro Bites*

## CHEERS!

You'll already have pale ale on hand for the empanadas, and those happen to work well with the whole menu, so you don't need to buy anything else to drink. Of course, you could always whip up some slushies with powdered drink mix, sugar, ice, and water (alcohol optional) in your blender, too.

# Shrimp Tacos

**SERVES 2 ♥ PREP TIME:** 5 MINUTES ♥ **COOK TIME:** 15 MINUTES
**30-MINUTE**

Shrimp are the perfect ingredient for a date-night meal because they cook so quickly. In this recipe, they require even less attention since everything's baked in the oven, letting you get to the relaxing part of the evening more quickly. These shrimp tacos are prepped in 5 minutes and cooked in less than 15 minutes. You can top them with sour cream, but avocado, sliced radishes, and cilantro are all delicious options, too.

Nonstick cooking spray

8 ounces shrimp, shelled, deveined, and tails removed

1 small red onion, sliced

1 cup frozen corn

1 teaspoon chili powder

½ teaspoon ground cumin

½ teaspoon garlic powder

¼ teaspoon salt

2 tablespoons extra-virgin olive oil

4 taco-size tortillas

Sour cream, for topping

1. Preheat the oven to 450°F. Line a baking sheet with aluminum foil and spray it with cooking spray.

2. In a large bowl, mix together the shrimp, onion, corn, chili powder, cumin, garlic powder, salt, and olive oil. Spread out the shrimp and vegetables on the prepared baking sheet.

3. Bake for 10 to 15 minutes, or until the shrimp are cooked through and the veggies are softened.

4. Wrap the tortillas in aluminum foil and put them in the oven for the last 4 minutes of baking time.

5. Place the shrimp and vegetables on the warm tortillas. Top with sour cream and enjoy.

**TIP:** You can use frozen peeled and deveined shrimp; just run them under cold water for a few minutes prior to preparing the dish.

**FOR THE SOUS-CHEF:** Measure the spices while the chef gets the shrimp and veggies into the bowl.

# Bean Empanadas

**SERVES 2 ♥ PREP TIME:** 10 MINUTES ♥ **COOK TIME:** 20 MINUTES

30-MINUTE, VEGETARIAN

Empanadas are a favorite in my house. In this version, we have creamy pinto beans (another favorite around here) instead of beef. You'll find frozen empanada discs in the international section of the frozen foods aisle. Defrost them in the refrigerator and keep them there until you're ready to add the filling. Empanadas are typically fried, but you can bake them and still get that iconic crunch.

- 1 tablespoon avocado oil
- 1 small green bell pepper, diced (about ¾ cup)
- ¼ cup diced onion
- 1 (14½-ounce) can pinto beans, rinsed and drained
- ⅓ cup raisins
- ⅓ cup beer (like a pale ale) or no-sodium-added vegetable stock
- 2 tablespoons tomato paste
- 2 garlic cloves, minced
- ½ teaspoon ground cumin
- ¼ teaspoon kosher salt
- ¼ teaspoon freshly ground black pepper
- 6 (5-inch) frozen empanada discs, thawed

1. In a medium skillet, heat the oil over medium heat until it shimmers. Add the bell pepper and onion and sauté for 2 minutes, until the vegetables have softened.

2. Stir in the beans, raisins, beer, tomato paste, garlic, cumin, salt, and black pepper. Bring to a simmer and cook for 3 to 4 minutes, until the beer has been reduced by half. Remove from the heat.

3. Meanwhile, preheat the oven to 450°F. Line a baking sheet with parchment paper.

4. Top each empanada disc with ¼ cup of the filling. Fold the empanadas in half and, using a fork, press the edges together to seal.

5. Arrange the stuffed empanadas in a single layer on the prepared baking sheet. Bake for 12 to 14 minutes, or until golden brown. Remove from the oven.

**FOR THE SOUS-CHEF:** While the chef works on steps 1 and 2, preheat the oven and line the baking sheet.

# Mini Churro Bites

**SERVES 2 OR 3 ♥ PREP TIME:** 10 MINUTES ♥ **COOK TIME:** 15 MINUTES

5-INGREDIENT, 30-MINUTE, VEGETARIAN

Don't worry, you don't have to start from scratch on these—that would take way too long. Refrigerated biscuit dough, cinnamon, and sugar combine to create this super tasty dessert! I am not a huge fan of frying things, but these require a little bit of oil to get them to golden-brown perfection. Since date night's always a special occasion, serve them with warm caramel sauce for an extra dose of decadence.

**1 cup vegetable oil**

**1 (6-ounce) package refrigerated biscuits**

**¼ cup sugar**

**1 teaspoon ground cinnamon**

**½ cup caramel sauce**

1. In a small saucepan, heat the oil over medium-high heat. (There should be about 1 inch of oil on the bottom of the pan.)

2. Cut the biscuit dough into 1-inch pieces.

3. In a small bowl, combine the sugar and cinnamon.

4. Drop four or five biscuit pieces into the hot oil and cook for 30 to 45 seconds. Using a slotted spoon, flip and cook for another 30 seconds, until golden brown. Immediately remove the biscuit pieces from the oil and transfer them to a paper towel–lined plate. Repeat with the remaining pieces of dough.

5. Working in batches, once the pieces are cool enough to touch, roll the churros in the bowl of cinnamon sugar.

6. In a small microwave-safe bowl, microwave the caramel sauce until warm. Dip the mini churro bites into the warm caramel sauce. Serve and enjoy.

**TIP:** These can also be baked. Preheat the oven to 350°F. Place the churro bites on a baking sheet and bake for 12 to 13 minutes, until lightly browned.

**FOR THE SOUS-CHEF:** While the chef heats the oil for frying and cuts the dough, mix the cinnamon and sugar. Then, while the chef works on frying the churro bites in batches, warm up the caramel sauce.

# ACTIVITY: Compliments from Around the World

Sometimes we neglect to speak our thoughts out loud when we admire something about our partner. Take a moment to gush about each other's admirable qualities—in other languages. Nothing's off-limits. Take time to really observe each other or say what you've been thinking all along.

**Supplies needed:** Internet connection and/or a translator app

**Estimated time:** 5 to 10 minutes

## INSTRUCTIONS

1.  Search for a website or app that will allow you to translate phrases from one language to another one of your choice. Think about something you'd like to compliment your partner on and type that into the translator. Read it aloud or play it from the website or app.

2.  Let your partner guess the compliment.

3.  Switch places, receive a compliment from your partner, and try to guess what it is.

4.  Who gave the most unique or most thoughtful compliment? Try funny and unexpected compliments and switch up the languages as often as you'd like. You'll both leave the activity feeling lighter, happier, and more appreciated.

5.  Try to do this once a week, every morning, or every night and make it a part of your daily routine.

6.  Transcribe your favorite compliments and the language on the following lines as a reminder of what you love about each other.

*Whipped Ricotta with Grilled Peaches,* **PAGE 129**

# CHAPTER FIVE

# A Date for Every Season

Mark the passing of time with your sweetheart by looking to the season for your date night inspiration. Spring and summer call for enjoying the sun together, while fall and winter offer an opportunity to get cozy and cuddle up. And with each dinner, you can take the time to stop and think about how far you've come together since the previous year.

# SPRINGTIME PICNIC

This is the perfect menu for those first warm days of the year, when you just want to walk to a local park or put a blanket down in the backyard. The sweet and spicy combination of recipes is both filling and refreshing, ideal for taking a time-out in the sunshine. Start with deviled eggs spiced up with hot sauce and cayenne, then enjoy a melon and cucumber salad along with hearty chicken salad sandwiches that have been amped up with pecans and cherries. There's even light, creamy cheesecake cups for a satisfying finishing touch.

## MENU

*Devilish Deviled Eggs*

*Melon and
Cucumber Salad*

*Cherry-Pecan Chicken
Salad Sandwiches*

*No-Bake Strawberry
Cheesecake Cups*

## CHEERS!

A picnic practically begs for a bottle of lemonade. Jazz it up with a (discreet) splash of gin or mix it with some club soda for festive bubbles. You could even drop some strawberry slices into your glasses.

# Devilish Deviled Eggs

**SERVES 2 ♥ PREP TIME:** 15 MINUTES ♥ **COOK TIME:** 15 MINUTES

30-MINUTE, VEGETARIAN

I love deviled eggs and can devour an embarrassing number of them in one sitting. I also love spicy food. The traditional deviled egg recipe meets cayenne pepper and sriracha here for a match made in heaven. Although deviled eggs are typically served to a crowd, there's no reason the two of you can't enjoy a small batch alone.

2 large eggs

1 tablespoon mayonnaise

1 teaspoon Dijon mustard

1 teaspoon hot sauce, such as sriracha

Salt

Freshly ground black pepper

Ground cayenne pepper, for garnish

½ teaspoon finely chopped fresh chives, for garnish

1. Fill a pot with enough water to cover the eggs and bring to a full boil. Boil, uncovered, for about 30 seconds. Reduce the heat to low and cover. Simmer for 12 minutes. Transfer the boiled eggs to a bowl of ice water. When the eggs are cool enough to handle, gently break the shells apart and peel.

2. Cut the boiled eggs in half. Separate the yolks from the whites using a teaspoon.

3. In a small bowl, combine the egg yolks, mayonnaise, mustard, and hot sauce and season with salt and black pepper. Fill a piping bag or resealable bag with the mixture, cut off one corner of the bag, and then squeeze the mixture into the egg white halves.

4. Garnish with sprinkles of cayenne pepper and chives to serve.

**TIP:** You can make deviled eggs up to 2 days in advance. Just store the whites and egg yolk filling separately. Wrap the egg white halves well with plastic wrap and keep the egg yolk filling sealed in a resealable plastic bag with all the air squeezed out until you are ready to assemble and serve.

**FOR THE SOUS-CHEF:** While the chef works on peeling and cutting the eggs, combine the rest of the ingredients for the filling.

# Melon and Cucumber Salad

**SERVES 2 ♥ PREP TIME:** 15 MINUTES

30-MINUTE, VEGETARIAN

This summery salad is light, crisp, and refreshing. The cucumber brings a bit of savory flavor to the dish, and the lime and mint brighten it up even more. Even though watermelon and cantaloupe are in it, it's not too sweet. If you make extra, you can have Date Night Part 2 on your patio tomorrow evening, so feel free to cube and slice extra watermelon, cantaloupe, and cucumber (mix other ingredients in later) if you'll have the time to relax outdoors tomorrow.

1 cup cubed cantaloupe

1 cup cubed watermelon

1 small cucumber, peeled and diced

Zest and juice of ½ lime

2 tablespoons chopped fresh mint

1 teaspoon extra-virgin olive oil

¼ cup feta cheese

1. In a medium bowl, combine the cantaloupe, watermelon, cucumber, lime zest, lime juice, mint, and olive oil and mix.

2. Top with the feta cheese. Serve and enjoy.

**TIP:** If you have a melon baller, you can use it here to creates perfect bite-size pieces (though cutting will work just as well).

**SWAP:** Honeydew or any other type of melon that you like will make an excellent substitution for the cantaloupe and watermelon.

**FOR THE SOUS-CHEF:** Help cut up the ingredients, then pour the drinks while your partner combines the ingredients.

# Cherry-Pecan Chicken Salad Sandwiches

**SERVES: 2** ♥ **PREP TIME:** 10 MINUTES ♥ **COOK TIME:** 10 MINUTES

30-MINUTE

I love chicken salad for a few reasons: It's versatile (eat it on bread, a croissant, on a bed of greens, or straight out of a bowl), it's portable and perfect for picnics, and it's delicious—and easy to augment with your favorite herbs, fruits, etc. In this recipe, the chicken is dressed up with a mix of nutty, earthy pecans and tart-sweet cherries; feel free to swap out ingredients, or add new ones, and make it your own.

2 boneless skinless chicken
    breasts
¼ cup mayonnaise
¼ cup plain Greek yogurt or sour
    cream
1 shallot, diced

1 celery stalk, diced
½ cup chopped pecans
¼ cup dried cherries
Salt
Freshly ground black pepper

1. Fill a medium pot halfway with water and place over high heat. As the water heats up, cut each chicken breast into two pieces. Add the chicken to the pot and boil until cooked through, about 10 minutes. Using tongs, remove the chicken from the water and shred or chop into bite-size pieces.

2. In a medium bowl, combine the chicken, mayonnaise, Greek yogurt, shallot, celery, pecans, and cherries. Season with salt and pepper. Serve and enjoy.

**TIP:** Use shredded rotisserie chicken to save yourself time.

**SWAP:** You can use dried cranberries instead of dried cherries or almonds instead of pecans.

**FOR THE SOUS-CHEF:** Work on the Melon and Cucumber Salad while your partner prepares the chicken salad.

# No-Bake Strawberry Cheesecake Cups

**SERVES 2 ♥ PREP TIME:** 15 MINUTES

30-MINUTE, VEGETARIAN

Strawberry cheesecake is one of my favorite desserts, and cheesecake is one of the few desserts my husband and I can agree on (he dislikes chocolate about as much as I like it . . . which is a *lot*). These are light enough to enjoy together after a big meal.

½ cup diced fresh strawberries

⅓ cup heavy (whipping) cream

4 ounces cream cheese, at room temperature

¼ cup powdered sugar

½ teaspoon vanilla extract

¼ cup graham cracker crumbs, plus more for serving

1. Put the strawberries in a blender or food processor and blend until very few chunks remain.

2. In a medium bowl, using an electric mixer on high, mix the heavy cream for about 2 minutes, until stiff peaks form. Set aside.

3. In another medium bowl, using an electric mixer on medium-high, beat the cream cheese, powdered sugar, and vanilla for about 2 minutes, until the mixture becomes fluffy. Add the strawberry puree and beat using the mixer until combined.

4. Gently fold the whipped cream into the strawberry cream cheese mixture.

5. Coat the bottom of two bowls or cups with the graham cracker crumbs. Top with the strawberry cheesecake mixture.

6. Top with additional graham cracker crumbs. Serve and enjoy.

**TIP:** To save yourself a little bit of prep time, use store-bought whipped cream instead of making it from scratch.

**FOR THE SOUS-CHEF:** While the chef works on step 1 to puree the strawberries, whip the cream. Then, as the chef mixes the ingredients in step 3 and 4, coat the bottoms of the bowls or cups with the graham cracker crumbs.

## ACTIVITY: Plan a Spring Break

Why should college kids have all the fun? Now that the cold of winter is gone, make a plan for enjoying some fun in the sun—even if it's just for a day or a weekend. Plan a future "break" (or a few of them!) by asking yourselves the following questions:

▸ What's the closest spot you can think of for an impromptu break? Can you fit a trip there into your calendar in the next few weeks?

▸ Relive the glory days or avoid them at all costs? Share your spring-break stories and create your grown-up spring-break profile.

▸ Can you carve out some time for a longer break? (Look up cheap plane fares and let the fates decide!)

# SUMMERTIME AND THE GRILLING IS EASY

If you look forward to peaches in the summer, this collection of recipes is for you. This quintessential summer fruit bookends the meal: You start with a sweet-savory gazpacho, where the peaches are paired up with melon, feta, fresh herbs, and jalapeño, and end with peaches that are grilled until they're slightly caramelized, then topped with sweet, whipped ricotta. And for the main? Grilled tuna steaks with a delectable, savory sesame crust offer a hearty, slightly upscale option for a perfect backyard cookout for two.

## MENU

*Savory Peach and Melon Gazpacho with Feta*

*Grilled Sesame-Crusted Tuna Steaks*

*Whipped Ricotta with Grilled Peaches*

## CHEERS!

A rosé makes a wonderful addition to this meal and carries the summertime vibe right into your glass. If you feel like being more adventurous, a white (or rosé, or mix of both) sangria with watermelon and peaches would be perfect. Feel like skipping the alcohol? What about fruit-infused sparkling water with a hint of mint?

# Savory Peach and Melon Gazpacho with Feta

**SERVES 2 ♥ PREP TIME:** 10 MINUTES

30-MINUTE, VEGETARIAN

This delightful, no-cook soup is the best balance of sweet, juicy, spicy, and salty. It'll also help use a huge honking melon that is taking up all of the room in your refrigerator. Since most of these ingredients will be going into a food processor, chop the watermelon and tomatoes just enough to fit them into your food processor.

1 peach, peeled, pitted, and cut into chunks

1 cup watermelon chunks

½ cup tomato chunks

½ cup cucumber chunks

2 tablespoons chopped red onion

1 teaspoon minced jalapeño pepper

1 teaspoon minced garlic

½ teaspoon salt, plus more as needed

5 fresh mint leaves

5 fresh basil leaves

1 tablespoon honey or maple syrup

1 tablespoon freshly squeezed lime juice

¼ cup extra-virgin olive oil

2 tablespoons crumbled feta cheese (optional)

Freshly ground black pepper

1. Put the peach, watermelon, tomato, cucumber, and onion in a food processor. Pulse until all of the ingredients are finely chopped and have released their juices. Scrape down the sides of the food processor bowl with a rubber spatula in between pulses, if needed.

2. Add the jalapeño pepper, garlic, salt, mint, basil, honey, and lime juice. Run the food processor while drizzling in the olive oil. Taste the gazpacho and season with more salt, if needed.

3. Serve the gazpacho with the feta (if using) and a few turns of pepper.

**FOR THE SOUS-CHEF:** This is a quick, one-person job once everything's cut up, so go ahead and pour a couple drinks to enjoy while you work on dinner. If you have two cutting boards, you can share the chopping task.

# Grilled Sesame-Crusted Tuna Steaks

**SERVES 2** ♥ **PREP TIME:** 20 MINUTES ♥ **COOK TIME:** 10 MINUTES

30-MINUTE

Seared tuna may seem like something you'd only get at restaurants, but it's surprisingly easy to prepare at home. This grilled tuna is marinated in a simple mixture of soy sauce, sesame oil, rice wine vinegar, and fresh ginger and then coated in sesame seeds. The steaks need only a couple minutes on the grill to be perfectly seared on the outside and rare on the inside. (Feel free to cook them longer if that makes you more comfortable.)

2 tablespoons soy sauce
1 tablespoon sesame oil
1 tablespoon rice wine vinegar
1 teaspoon minced fresh ginger

2 (6-ounce) tuna steaks
¼ cup sesame seeds
2 tablespoons chopped scallions, green part only

1. In a medium bowl, whisk together the soy sauce, sesame oil, rice wine vinegar, and ginger. Put the tuna steaks in a small plastic container and pour the mixture over them. Let it sit for 10 minutes.

2. Preheat the grill to medium-high heat.

3. Remove the steaks from the container and place them on a flat surface. Press the sesame seeds into the tuna steaks.

4. Put the tuna steaks on the grill and cook for 2 to 3 minutes on each side, depending on your preference of doneness, watching the steaks closely.

5. Top the tuna with the scallions. Serve and enjoy.

**TIP:** This recipe creates tuna with a rare center. For a medium-rare center, cook for 1 to 2 minutes more on each side.

**FOR THE SOUS-CHEF:** Make the marinade while the chef removes the tuna steaks from their packaging and gets the grill ready.

# Whipped Ricotta with Grilled Peaches

**SERVES 2 ♥ PREP TIME:** 15 MINUTES ♥ **COOK TIME:** 5 MINUTES

5-INGREDIENT, 30-MINUTE, VEGETARIAN

Even with desserts, sometimes the simplest ingredient goes a long way. Just five minutes on the grill transforms peaches from a snack to an irresistible dessert that's perfect for an outdoor setting on a warm night because it's sweet but not too heavy. The ricotta cheese feels sophisticated when it's whipped with heavy cream, honey, and vanilla, but it's really quite simple. If you're feeling really fancy, you can top this dish off with a sprig of mint.

½ cup whole-milk ricotta cheese
2 tablespoons heavy (whipping) cream

2 tablespoons honey, divided
1 teaspoon vanilla extract
2 peaches, halved and pitted

1. Preheat the grill to medium heat.

2. In a small bowl, whip together the ricotta cheese, heavy cream, 1 tablespoon of honey, and the vanilla.

3. Brush the flesh side of the peaches with the remaining 1 tablespoon of honey. On well-greased grates, grill the peaches, flesh-side down, for 4 to 5 minutes, until you see grill marks.

4. Top the peaches with a dollop of the whipped ricotta cheese. Serve and enjoy.

**SWAP:** Any kind of stone fruit will work in this recipe, including nectarines, plums, and apricots.

**FOR THE SOUS-CHEF:** Prepare the ricotta cheese mixture in step 2 while the chef grills the peaches.

## ACTIVITY: A Fill-in-the-Blanks Story

This activity will hopefully inspire some laughs as you work together to create a zany micro-story. Who knows what direction you'll take this in together! You can repeat it as often as you'd like—the story will be different every time.

**Supplies needed:** Pen or pencil

**Estimated time:** 5 minutes

### INSTRUCTIONS

1. Decide which one of you will be the one to see the story ahead of time. Don't let your partner see the story before all the blanks are filled!

2. That person will call out each word prompt listed under each blank line, in order. Allow your partner to speak what comes to mind and write it down in the corresponding blank space.

3. Read the letter out loud at the end once all the blanks are filled.

## SUMMERTIME AND THE GRILLING IS EASY

Dear _____,
  name of partner with the book right now

I am SO _____ we met at _____ when we did that
         emotion (adjective)              place

_____ in the _____. My life has been
      activity                      season

full of _____ and _____ since then. And to think that
       emotion (noun)        emotion (noun)

when I woke up that morning, I was in such a _____ mood. It was
                                            emotion (adjective)

so nice to find someone to talk about _____ with! I felt like you
                                         topic

totally _____ me. Here's something I've never told you: The
       verb, past tense

_____ I wore that day is now my lucky _____. Now I always
article of clothing                              article of clothing

wear it when I _____. I can't wait for the day when we _____
               verb                                               verb

together. My favorite memory so far is when we _____ at _____.
                                               verb, past tense      place

You were so _____! Did you think I was _____? I sure hope so.
            verb, past tense                       adjective

Sincerely,

_____
name of partner without the book right now

P.S. On our next date, we should go out for _____ and watch _____.
                                             food                      movie

I'll wear my _____ _____ and maybe you can wear
             color            article of clothing

your _____ _____.
     color            article of clothing

# FALLING FOR COMFORT FOOD

Comfort foods are good any time of year, but they're especially delicious when the days start getting shorter and the nights start getting cooler. This menu (which is ideal right around Halloween), lets you settle in for some ghost stories and a filling meal with a sweet treat at the end. The meatloaf will take about an hour to cook, so while it's on the oven, you'll have plenty of time to enjoy each other's company and talk about ghosts, the afterlife, and haunted locations you've been dying to visit. If the sous-chef preps the pinwheels while the chef gets the meatloaf in the oven, you'll have even more free time.

## MENU

*Stuffed Meatloaf with Spicy Roasted Cauliflower*

*Garlic-Herb Pinwheels*

*Peanut Butter Cup Shakes*

*Old-Fashioned*

## CHEERS!

If you want to skip the old-fashioneds, you could wash the meatloaf and sides down with a nice cold glass of sweet tea, but a merlot or Pinot Noir may feel more special and less like a family dinner. Red wines tie in well with the cozy fall/winter vibe here, too.

# Stuffed Meatloaf with Spicy Roasted Cauliflower

**SERVES 4** ♥ **PREP TIME:** 15 MINUTES ♥ **COOK TIME:** 1 HOUR

If meatloaf sounds more like off-putting mystery meat from the school lunchroom than a date-night dish, you're about to be pleasantly surprised. This tender, juicy, umami-filled beef ribboned with greens and complemented by notes of caramelized onions is the comfort food you didn't know you needed. You can substitute turkey, pork, bison, or chicken—any ground meat will do—though it might change the cooking time slightly. Can't find collards? Choose another hearty, leafy green to use in their place.

## FOR THE MEATLOAF

- 1½ teaspoons extra-virgin olive oil
- ½ yellow onion, diced
- 1 bunch collard greens, stemmed and chopped
- Pinch salt, plus ¼ teaspoon
- 1 pound ground beef
- 1 tablespoon Dijon mustard, plus 1 teaspoon
- 1 tablespoon ketchup, plus 1 teaspoon
- 1 tablespoon maple syrup
- 1½ teaspoons balsamic vinegar
- 1½ teaspoons tamari or soy sauce
- 1 large egg
- ½ cup panko bread crumbs (or gluten-free bread crumbs)
- Freshly ground black pepper

## FOR THE CAULIFLOWER

- 1 cauliflower head, broken into florets
- 1½ teaspoons avocado oil
- ¼ teaspoon salt
- ¼ teaspoon chili powder
- Pinch ground cumin
- Pinch paprika

1. **To make the meatloaf:** Preheat the oven to 350°F. Line a baking sheet with parchment paper.

2. In a medium skillet, heat the oil over medium heat. Add the onion and collard greens with a pinch of salt. Cook for about 10 minutes, or until the onion is caramelized. Remove from the heat. Set aside to cool.

CONTINUED >>

**Stuffed Meatloaf with Spicy Roasted Cauliflower** CONTINUED

3. In a large mixing bowl, combine the beef, cooled onion and collard greens, 1 tablespoon of mustard, 1 tablespoon of ketchup, the maple syrup, balsamic vinegar, tamari, egg, bread crumbs, and ¼ teaspoon of salt. Season with pepper. Mix until just combined. Be careful not to overmix.

4. Dump the meat mixture onto the prepared baking sheet and gently form an oval-shaped loaf, making a slight dent in the center that will help the center cook as quickly as the edges of the loaf.

5. In a small mixing bowl, mix the remaining 1 teaspoon of mustard and 1 teaspoon of ketchup. Brush over the top and sides of the loaf.

6. **To make the cauliflower:** In a separate large mixing bowl, combine the cauliflower, oil, salt, chili powder, cumin, and paprika. Toss until coated and scatter on the same baking sheet as the meatloaf, leaving plenty of room so the florets will roast and get some color rather than steam. Transfer the baking sheet to the oven and bake for 30 minutes.

7. Stir the cauliflower and rotate the baking sheet. Bake for another 10 to 20 minutes, or until the cauliflower is fork-tender and takes on a bit of color. The meatloaf should be at least 165°F in the center. Remove from the oven.

**FOR THE SOUS-CHEF:** Go ahead and prep the garlic-herb pinwheels while the chef prepares the meatloaf. You can pop those into the oven a little later.

*Garlic-Herb
Pinwheels,*
**PAGE 136**

# Garlic-Herb Pinwheels

**MAKES 18 PINWHEELS** ♥ **PREP TIME:** 40 MINUTES ♥ **COOK TIME:** 15 MINUTES

5-INGREDIENT, ONE POT, VEGETARIAN

Pinwheels . . . don't these sound fun to make (and eat)? You can make extras and have a delightful grab-and-go snack on hand for several days. Store them in an airtight container at room temperature and you'll be enjoying the leftovers from date night long after it's over. These are light and fresh in flavor, making them the perfect balance to the sweet, savory, and spicy elements of the main dish.

¼ cup mixed fresh herbs, such as parsley, basil, and chives

2 garlic cloves, minced

2 tablespoons unsalted butter, melted

Salt

Freshly ground black pepper

All-purpose flour, for dusting

1 frozen puff pastry sheet, thawed but still cold

1 tablespoon grated Parmesan cheese

1. In a small bowl, combine the fresh herbs, garlic, and butter. Season with salt and pepper.

2. On a lightly floured work surface, unfold the puff pastry. Spread the butter mixture evenly over the dough. Sprinkle the puff pastry with the Parmesan cheese. Roll up tightly to make a log and place in the freezer for 10 to 15 minutes.

3. Preheat the oven to 400°F.

4. Line a baking sheet with parchment paper.

5. With a sharp knife, cut the log into ½-inch-thick rounds. Arrange the rounds on the prepared baking sheet and bake for about 15 minutes, until puffed and the edges are golden. Let cool for 10 minutes before serving.

**TIP:** Take these pinwheels to another level by adding some thinly sliced prosciutto on top of the Parmesan before rolling up.

**FOR THE SOUS-CHEF:** You're in charge of putting these together while the chef works on the meatloaf. Don't put them in the oven right away, though.

# Peanut Butter Cup Shakes

**SERVES 2** ♥ **PREP TIME:** 5 MINUTES

5-INGREDIENT, 30-MINUTE, ONE POT, VEGETARIAN

The two of you go together like peanut butter and . . . chocolate! This is a quick and easy shake you can make and customize to your preferences. Love chunks of brownie, cookies, or extra peanut butter cups? Stir them into yours or sprinkle them on top. Are you a purist who prefers your shakes smooth and creamy? Skip the extras. This shake can please you both.

3 cups chocolate ice cream

⅔ cup milk

3 tablespoons creamy
   peanut butter

8 mini peanut butter cups, plus
   4 more chopped cups

1. In a blender, combine the ice cream, milk, and peanut butter and blend on high speed until combined.

2. Add the peanut butter cups to the blender and pulse until blended.

3. Divide between two glasses and top with the chopped peanut butter cups. Serve and enjoy.

**SWAP:** The chocolate ice cream and peanut butter cups can make for a very rich treat. If you want to keep the flavors on the lighter side, swap in vanilla ice cream. Chocolate sandwich cookies also work well here, too, in place of the peanut butter cups.

**FOR THE SOUS-CHEF:** Gather any additional toppings you may like while the chef blends.

# Old-Fashioned

**SERVES 2 ♥ PREP TIME:** 5 MINUTES

5-INGREDIENT, 30-MINUTE, VEGAN

The old-fashioned, which first appeared in the 1800s and was referred to as "bittered sling," is a classic cocktail. This simple blend of spirit, sweetener, and bitters is both timeless and delicious. It's an excellent way to play with a new bottle of any spirit, especially bourbon or rye whiskey.

**4 ounces bourbon or rye whiskey**
**½ ounce simple syrup**

**4 dashes Angostura bitters**
**Orange peels, for garnish**

1. In a mixing glass, combine the bourbon, simple syrup, and bitters.

2. Fill three-quarters of the glass with ice.

3. Stir until chilled, about 30 seconds.

4. Strain the drink into rocks glasses filled with ice (or one large cube).

5. Express the orange peels by twisting them over the drink and then running the peel along the inside rim of the glass. Drop the peel into the drink to garnish.

**FOR THE SOUS-CHEF:** Prepare the rocks glasses while your partner mixes the drinks or just take this whole task while your partner works on the meatloaf.

## ACTIVITY: **Spooky Dating**

Embrace darker nights by spending some time enjoying the macabre. It's fine to look some ghost stories up together if you don't have your own creepy tales to tell—maybe you'll even be inspired to invent your own (after all, *Frankenstein* was actually written as part of a party game)!

**Supplies needed:** Internet connection (optional)

**Estimated time:** 30+ minutes

### INSTRUCTIONS

If you have a spooky, scary, paranormal, and/or creepy story to tell, recount it to your partner. If they have one, too, have them tell theirs next. Once you're all out of stories (or if you don't have any to share), you can look some up online and read them together. You may even find some local tales tied to some of the sites near you that you can check out later.

Talk to your partner about what they believe about an afterlife. Do they believe in ghosts? If so, why do they think they're earthbound? Would they be scared to have an encounter with a ghost?

# COLD NIGHTS, SPICY FOOD

Personally, I'm a huge fan of spicy food any time of year, but the experience is just different in the winter, when you're freezing and then take a bite of a dish with some major kick to it. With these spicy chicken bites, zingy clam and corn chowder, and an El Diablo to drink (plus snuggling up to your significant other, of course!), you'll warm right up in no time. Then light a fire in the fireplace if you have one, and have some fun creating an indoor camping trip complete with s'mores (made in the microwave or oven, if needed).

## MENU

*Spicy Chicken Bites*

*Spicy Clam and Corn Chowder*

*El Diablo*

## CHEERS!

If you choose not to make the El Diablo, beer is a classic pairing for spicy food, as the bubbles help offset the heat. Lemonade is a refreshing option that will play well off the heat in these dishes, so you could switch things up and have that instead.

# Spicy Chicken Bites

**SERVES 2 ♥ PREP TIME:** 30 MINUTES ♥ **COOK TIME:** 15 MINUTES

### 5-INGREDIENT

Nothing says "quick bite" like chicken nuggets, but these aren't the frozen nuggets from your youth. Since it's date night, you can sit a little longer and savor every bite. (Tuck this recipe away for later, though, since these chicken bites are perfect for snacks, lunches, and salad toppers.)

| | |
|---|---|
| **1 boneless, skinless chicken breast, cubed** | **¼ teaspoon paprika** |
| **¼ cup extra-virgin olive oil** | **Dash cayenne pepper** |
| **2 garlic cloves, minced** | **Sea salt** |
| **¼ cup unseasoned bread crumbs** | **Freshly ground black pepper** |

1. In a large bowl, combine the chicken, olive oil, and garlic and toss to coat evenly. Cover and let marinate for 20 minutes.

2. Preheat the oven to 475°F. Line a baking sheet with aluminum foil and set aside.

3. In another large bowl, stir together the bread crumbs, paprika, and cayenne pepper. Season with salt and black pepper. Add the chicken and toss to coat.

4. Spread the chicken in a single layer on the prepared baking sheet and bake for 10 to 15 minutes, flipping halfway through the cooking time, until golden brown and crisp.

**FOR THE SOUS-CHEF:** After the chicken has marinated, preheat the oven and line the baking sheet with aluminum foil. Then start chopping the ingredients for the clam and corn chowder.

# Spicy Clam and Corn Chowder

**SERVES 2** ♥ **PREP TIME:** 15 MINUTES ♥ **COOK TIME:** 25 MINUTES

ONE POT

This chowder can keep you warm on cold, rainy days, and it also makes a wonderful summer soup. It's creamy yet light, spicy, and packed with delicious sweet corn and clams. Plus, everything tastes better with bacon!

- 4 bacon slices, chopped
- 1 large russet potato, cut into 1-inch pieces
- 2 tablespoons seafood seasoning, such as Old Bay seasoning
- 2 bay leaves
- 2 garlic cloves, chopped
- ¼ cup finely chopped jalapeño peppers

- 5 cups chicken stock
- 1 cup heavy (whipping) cream
- ½ cup chopped clams, canned or fresh, cleaned
- 2 cups frozen corn kernels, thawed
- Salt
- Freshly ground black pepper

1. In a Dutch oven, cook the bacon over low heat until crispy, about 10 minutes. Remove the bacon, leaving the grease in the pot.

2. Add the potato, increase the heat to medium, and cook, stirring occasionally, for 6 to 8 minutes, or until tender. Add the seafood seasoning, bay leaves, garlic, and jalapeño peppers and cook, stirring occasionally, for 3 to 5 minutes.

3. Stir in the stock and heavy cream. Bring to a simmer over medium-high heat. Add the clams and corn and stir to combine; cook until hot, about 3 minutes. Season with salt and black pepper. Remove the bay leaves.

4. Serve in individual bowls with the bacon crumbled on top.

**FOR THE SOUS-CHEF:** While the chef cooks the bacon, chop the potato, garlic, and jalapeño peppers, then gather the remaining ingredients.

# El Diablo

**SERVES 2 ♥ PREP TIME:** 5 MINUTES

5-INGREDIENT, 30-MINUTE, VEGAN

The El Diablo is thought to have been invented by famed tiki cocktail creator Victor "Trader Vic" Bergeron in the 1940s. The combination of fruity black currant liqueur, lime juice, and spicy ginger beer pairs perfectly with tequila in this refreshing cocktail. It's the perfect sweet and spicy combo to serve with this meal, and it works any time of the year.

**4 ounces tequila**

**1½ ounces freshly squeezed lime juice**

**1 ounce crème de cassis**

**8 ounces ginger beer**

**Lime wedges, for garnish**

1. Combine the tequila, lime juice, and crème de cassis in a cocktail shaker.

2. Fill the shaker three-quarters full with ice cubes and shake for about 12 seconds, or until chilled.

3. Fill highball glasses with ice cubes.

4. Strain the liquid into the glasses and top with the ginger beer.

5. Garnish with lime wedges.

**FOR THE SOUS-CHEF:** Once the chef takes over the last few steps of the deviled eggs, this drink-mixing project is all yours.

## ACTIVITY: Go Camping . . . Indoors!

Take this opportunity to re-create the fun of a night spent in the great outdoors—without leaving your living room! While some things may require a device, try to keep this experience as distraction-free as possible—just as if you'd set up a tent in the middle of the woods.

**Supplies needed:** Sleeping bags (optional)
Night sky projector (optional)
Favorite music or nature sounds
Ghost stories to share (you could make them up on the fly, find them online, or grab a book and a flashlight)
Microwave
Chocolate bar
Jumbo marshmallows
Graham crackers

**Estimated time:** 2 hours to most (or all) of the night

### INSTRUCTIONS

1. Set up your sleeping bags if you're using them.
2. Project the night sky onto the ceiling, if you like.
3. Find a playlist of your favorite songs or really add to the outdoor camping experience with a playlist of nature sounds.
4. Turn off the lights and snuggle up with your special someone.
5. Listen to the sounds of nature or your favorite tunes, tell some ghost stories, and pop out to the "campfire" (a.k.a. the microwave) to make s'mores. See where the conversation takes you as you gaze up at the stars.

# Measurement Conversions

| VOLUME EQUIVALENTS | US STANDARD | US STANDARD (OUNCES) | METRIC (APPROXIMATE) |
|---|---|---|---|
| **LIQUID** | 2 tablespoons | 1 fl. oz. | 30 mL |
| | ¼ cup | 2 fl. oz. | 60 mL |
| | ½ cup | 4 fl. oz. | 120 mL |
| | 1 cup | 8 fl. oz. | 240 mL |
| | 1½ cups | 12 fl. oz. | 355 mL |
| | 2 cups or 1 pint | 16 fl. oz. | 475 mL |
| | 4 cups or 1 quart | 32 fl. oz. | 1 L |
| | 1 gallon | 128 fl. oz. | 4 L |
| **DRY** | ⅛ teaspoon | – | 0.5 mL |
| | ¼ teaspoon | – | 1 mL |
| | ½ teaspoon | – | 2 mL |
| | ¾ teaspoon | – | 4 mL |
| | 1 teaspoon | – | 5 mL |
| | 1 tablespoon | – | 15 mL |
| | ¼ cup | – | 59 mL |
| | ⅓ cup | – | 79 mL |
| | ½ cup | – | 118 mL |
| | ⅔ cup | – | 156 mL |
| | ¾ cup | – | 177 mL |
| | 1 cup | – | 235 mL |
| | 2 cups or 1 pint | – | 475 mL |
| | 3 cups | – | 700 mL |
| | 4 cups or 1 quart | – | 1 L |
| | ½ gallon | – | 2 L |
| | 1 gallon | – | 4 L |

### OVEN TEMPERATURES

| FAHRENHEIT | CELSIUS (APPROXIMATE) |
|---|---|
| 250°F | 120°C |
| 300°F | 150°C |
| 325°F | 165°C |
| 350°F | 180°C |
| 375°F | 190°C |
| 400°F | 200°C |
| 425°F | 220°C |
| 450°F | 230°C |

### WEIGHT EQUIVALENTS

| US STANDARD | METRIC (APPROXIMATE) |
|---|---|
| ½ ounce | 15 g |
| 1 ounce | 30 g |
| 2 ounces | 60 g |
| 4 ounces | 115 g |
| 8 ounces | 225 g |
| 12 ounces | 340 g |
| 16 ounces or 1 pound | 455 g |

# Resources

If you need some help with the basics of cooking and some general kitchen tips before you feel comfortable making your own dinner during date night, check out the "How-Tos" section of TheSpruceEats.com.

If you prefer videos when you're learning new cooking techniques and tricks, try Serious Eats on YouTube.

For a similar learning experience when it comes to mixology (which will be useful when you get ready to create your Couple's Cocktail), visit DrinkSkool.com. You'll find other drinks to try there, too, which may be helpful when you don't have all the ingredients on hand to make the recommended drink on a menu.

If you really want to go all in like I did when I decided to stop being afraid in the kitchen and learn how to cook, working your way through *The Whole 30: The 30-Day Guide to Total Health and Food Freedom* can help you get there. You don't have to do a round of Whole 30 to use the book, but that's how I forced myself to learn so much in a short period of time. I gave myself no choice but to get outside my comfort zone.

# Index

# ACKNOWLEDGMENTS

Thank you to my husband for always being ready to cook dinner or go pick up the takeout I asked him to order (since not every night can be date night in) and to my daughter for supplying many pots of "afternoon coffee" as I worked to meet deadlines and conquer the desperate need for a nap simultaneously. Thank you to my editor, Cecily, for patiently answering all my questions (even the ones I realized were silly after I hit Send) and to the whole Callisto team for working together with me on this book.

# ABOUT THE AUTHOR

 **Crystal Schwanke** is a freelance writer, a lifestyle blogger, and the author of *The Couple's Activity Book*. She lives in the Atlanta, Georgia, area with her husband, daughter, and perpetually skeptical pit bull named Josephine. When she's not writing, testing something new (for a review or to satisfy her own curiosity), or researching her latest obsession, she enjoys escaping into historical fiction, making up silly songs, reading about psychology, and consuming massive amounts of coffee. You can visit her site at ThatOldKitchenTable.com.